Harriet Beecher Stowe: Woman and Artist

OTHER BOOKS BY EDWARD M. HOLMES

Faulkner's Twice-Told Tales:
His Re-Use of His Material
Driftwood
A Part of the Main
Mostly Maine

Edward M. Holmes

Harriet Beecher Stowe
Woman and Artist

with a Foreword by Josephine Donovan

NORTHERN LIGHTS
Orono, Maine 1991

Northern Lights, Inc.
493 College Avenue
Orono, Maine 04473

cover design by Michael Fournier

ISBN: 0-9621570-4-X
Library of Congress Card Catalog Number: 91-67181

CONTENTS

GALLERY

(appearing after page 135)

FOREWORD

Ellen Moers once remarked how critics and scholars repeatedly "rediscover" the novels of Harriet Beecher Stowe, registering anew surprise and pleasure at their richness, variety, and power (*New York Review of Books*, 3 September 1970). Edmund Wilson, for example, found reading *Uncle Tom's Cabin* "a startling experience." It was, he said, "a much more impressive work than one has ever been allowed to suspect." The same is true of Stowe's other fiction, particularly the great "local color" novels of the 1860s: *The Minister's Wooing* (1859), *The Pearl of Orr's Island* (1862), and *Oldtown Folks* (1869).

Perhaps Stowe is burdened by her "Eminent Woman" stature: the dour image projected in various portraits may negatively influence readers' expectations. We have a tendency to consign great women of the past to a "Whistler's Mother," rocking-chair status; this may be why we expect Stowe's novels to be dull and reading them an academic chore.

Edward Holmes's is the latest attempt to awaken readers to the intellectual pleasures and excitement of Stowe's fictional world. His study, written in accessible, lively, and jargon-free prose, should motivate common readers to seek out these remarkable works. Holmes commonsensically and realistically places Stowe firmly in the context of her historical moment. Here, perhaps more clearly than in previous studies, we get a sense of how Stowe must have experienced life intellectually. The ideological strains that run through Stowe's work are often contradictory. Holmes singles out sentimentalism, realism, Calvinism, and romanticism. At different times and in different works one or the other may predominate, but all are present to some degree in all her work.

Holmes is correct, I think, to stress, however, that Stowe's sentimentalism is only skin-deep. It is true that she uses sentimentalist devices and plots, but in her heart as I have argued elsewhere, she is a realist. By that I (and Holmes) mean that she usually took a critical view of received myth; indeed she could be quite cynical and her wit quite sarcastic—something one never finds in the sentimentalists.

It is doubtful that Stowe cared to iron out the contradictions in her world views. She clearly wrote rapidly and carelessly. In an 1864 letter to her publisher, James T. Fields, Harriet asked that his wife, Annie (probably Stowe's closest friend), do a substantial job of editing an article she has submitted. "Dear Friend Fields. . .Please let Annie loot it over &. . .make it right. If Annie thinks of any other thing that ought to be mentioned & will put it in for me she will serve both the cause and me" (as cited in *James C. Austin, Fields of the Atlantic Monthly: Letters to an Editor,* 1861—70 [San Marino, Calif.: Huntington Library, 1953], pp. 277-78).

What she did care about where matters of social justice. Her concerns extended to all the oppressed of society—black slaves, women, the poor, even animals. Indeed, her tract "Rights of Dumb Animals" (*Hearth and Home* 2, January 1869), which could stand as an "animal rights" statement today, is moving evidence of the extent of her compassion and the depth of her sense of justice. The ambivalences inherent in Stowe's fictional work, however, have caused readers to interpret and evaluate it variously depending on which facet they see. Sarah Orne Jewett, for example, who claimed Stowe as a primary influence, changed her mind about *The Pearl of Orr's Island* several times. In her 1893 (second) preface to *Deephaven* Jewett noted:

> It was, happily, in the writer's childhood that Mrs. Stowe had written of those who dwelt along the wooded seacoast and by the decaying, shipless harbors of Maine. The first chapters of *The Pearl of Orr's Island* gave the young author of *Deephaven* to see with new eyes, and to follow eagerly the old shore paths from one gray, weather-beaten house to another where Genius pointed the way.

Later, however, Jewett complained that the novel lacked integrity because, she implied, Stowe had written it too carelessly.

"Alas, that she couldn't finish it in the same noble key of simplicity and harmony; but a poor writer is at the mercy of much unconscious opposition. You must throw everything and everybody aside at times, but a woman made like Mrs. Stowe cannot bring herself to that cold selfishness of the moment for one's works sake, and the recompense for her loss is a divine touch here and there in an incomplete piece of work" (*Letters of Sarah Orne Jewett*, ed. Annie Fields [Boston: Houghton Mifflin, 1911], p. 47).

Still later (in an unpublished letter now in the Houghton Library, Harvard University) Jewett recanted the above criticism, returning to her earlier enthusiasm.

All Jewett's reactions are valid. Stowe's works are not structurally perfect nor ideologically consistent; but the "divine touches"—her shrewd perceptions of character, her energetic and realistic descriptions, her panoramic settings, and the palpable passion for justice that animates her best work—countervail. Harriet Beecher Stowe remains one of our great writers.

Josephine Donovan
Portsmouth, New Hampshire

INTRODUCTION

Invariably the old gods die lingering and painful deaths. Although their passing is often not even recognized until after they have gone, persons who are involved in the dwindling process, who are losing former world-views, or, all unwittingly, are helping to kill them, know an anxiety and turmoil that is sometimes peculiar to their epoch. Such was the position of Harriet Beecher Stowe in the three decades following 1850.

The impact of the ideas of Jean-Jacques Rousseau, of German idealism, and of the Declaration of Independence, among other documents and writings, took their toll, in time, of the philosophy and theology that Jonathan Edwards had striven so mightily to rejuvenate in the eighteenth century. After 1818, Congregationalism was no longer the established religion of the State of Connecticut. Unitarianism came to flourish in Boston, and the Hub honored and listened to William Ellery Channing. Emerson resigned his New England pastorate, and withdrawing to a Concord home, wrote: "As men's prayers are a disease of the will, so are their creeds a disease of the intellect." Transcendentalism spawned lectures, discussions, and articles in the *Dial*. Brook Farm and Fruitlands came to an end; Webster made

---

his Seventh of March speech to the Senate; and Whittier penned "Ichabod." To the stricken conscience and horror of the North, the Fugitive Slave Bill became law.

Whereas formerly some men had lived in the hope they might, possibly, be among the elect, and should in any case live to the greater glory of God, now, almost suddenly, the gates of Heaven were open wider. Perfectibility was no longer the monopoly of a handful of saints, and reform and improvement, the seeds of which had been planted in the nation at its very start, became, for purposes of salvation, as important as, if not more important than repentance and submission to the will of God. Oliver Wendell Holmes allegorized in "The Wonderful One-Hoss Shay," the termination of Calvinism as a living force, and then, in such novels as *Elsie Venner*, searched for a physiological Absolute, a replacement of some kind for what he sensed was lost.

The American world, following a decade of debate, spun into the Civil War, a time of paid substitutes and profits, as well as of sacrifice and liberation, and in the years that followed, no small number of Americans became over-burdened with an exaggerated lust for unearned wealth. The seventies were in many ways an unlovely sight, as had been many of the feverish years before them.

These were the decades in which Mrs. Stowe wrote. She had been born in a world almost eighteenth century in spirit, and she lived to within a few years of the twentieth. Often in her books she looked back, loving, liking, and also not liking what she had lost;

frequently, since she was not one to inhabit towers, she looked around her, and a short way ahead, seldom pleased at what she discovered, but never without hope.

A reading of her novels yields, to this critic, an awareness of four general elements, sometimes incongruous, and often in conflict, at work within her books. One conflict in particular is at the root of the best of her art. For want of better labels, the elements are here called, and named roughly in order of importance in her work, romanticism, a Puritan outlook, a sense of realism, and sentimentalism.

Following the description in chapter I of the literary and national environment in which she lived and in which her work grew, chapters II, III, and IV constitute an attempt to document the existence in her novels of the four characteristics named above. Chapter V offers a discussion of their effect on her books, with special emphasis on the conflict that produced her artistically most significant novels.

Charles H. Foster in *The Rungless Ladder*, has thoroughly traced the influence of Calvinism on the life and writings of Stowe, and Herbert Ross Brown, in *The Sentimental Novel in America*, has touched on her frequent indulgence in sentimental writing. More recent critics, such as Josephine Donovan, in *New England Local Color Literature*; Mary Kelley, in *Private Woman, Public Stage*; and Jane Tompkins, in *Sensational Designs*, offer a new perspective on the significance of the style and content of early and mid-nineteenth century fiction, including Stowe's.

The aim of this book is to show some additional

forces effective in her work, as well as those already sifted out, and to add evidence for supporting the claim that her novels are worth more attention than a century of inferior dramatizations of her most influential book would lead discriminating readers to think.

I. THE CONTEMPORARY CLOUD

The literary and social environment surrounding any writer is such a changing, various thing, a thing of multiple levels and numerous crosscurrents, that when we ask, "Whence came these forces?" when, for example, we say, "Why was there a great surge of the sentimental around, and beneath, and through the times of Harriet Beecher Stowe?" we find ourselves pushing back decade beyond decade, and very nearly century beyond century, in pursuit of first origins. We never find them, of course, but here and there we notice possibly significant conditions which look like the beginning of something, or the end of something, or both.

Life in the American Colonies was not easy. In winter, for the northern part of the country at least, it was hard. Standing wood may have been plentiful, but trees still had to be cut down, limbed, sawed, brought home, split perhaps, and at last carried in to a fire, an exhausting way, but the only way, of keeping warm. Who, other than the rich, would heat more than one room, and that the kitchen where the cook had to have fire in any event? For half the year, then, there was little privacy, and for the women there was a life even more thoroughly restricted than it was in summer.

Treating of Salem Village in 1692, Marion

Starkey writes:

> . . . . winter was dull. . . .The Puritan calendar
> provided no alleviation for the tedium of winter; such
> pagan festivities as Christmas and Mardi Gras, the
> one a splendid defiance against the death of light, and
> the other a heady foretaste of spring, were fiercely
> forbidden. . . .
> Womenfolk were not idle . . . but their activity was
> the same monotonous round they had known the year
> long . . . . In winter, every one of their scanty
> diversions was cut off. But for Sabbath meeting some
> of them would hardly have got out of the house at all.[1]

Assuredly Salem Village was not the American
Colonies, although it must have been like a
considerable part of them. Still, it was not Boston, or
Philadelphia, or New York, and as the eighteenth
century unrolled, life in America grew a little less
severe, a trifle less unrestricted for women; and this
was important too, because it provided some leisure in
which to read, a skill that was becoming increasingly
widespread.

Men discovered outlets for creative impulse in
numerous ways. Jonathan Edwards found expression
in theology and in sermons; Jefferson, in politics,
architecture, and gadgets; Washington, in war as well
as in statesmanship; Franklin, in nearly everything he
could see or touch. Others built ships, designed them,
or sailed them; still more turned their energies to a
craft or to trade. Women had the home.

Precisely, just as they had had it a half-century,
or a century before, and the home, every bit as much
as the rest of life, if not more than it, lived under the

---

1. Marion L. Starkey, *The Devil in Massachusetts*, New York, Alfred A. Knopf, 1950, pp. 11-12.

Harriet Beecher Stowe:

spell (the word is chosen advisedly, for not every age has the privilege of so thorough a conviction)—the spell of a Calvinist world view, which was also an after-world view. This outlook, not the ludicrously sober-sided affair of some twentieth century commentaries, but an earnest, profoundly sincere, intense *Anschauung*, habituated entire communities to following the tortuous, logical hair-splitting of Sabbath sermons, to probing the soul, in an examination of motives, for unrepented sin, and on occasion, to probing with like seriousness of intent, the souls of neighbors.

> With many New England women at this particular period, when life was so retired and cut off from outward sources of excitement, *thinking* grew to be a disease.[2]

Thus thoroughly and unwittingly did history prepare a society of novel readers, and furthermore, readers who would demand and absorb, in almost unlimited quantities, domestic themes.

Given generations of women subjected to tedium and activity only in the home, given generations of both sexes trained in religious introspection, is it any wonder that an emotional atmosphere beneath the surface, one that depth psychologists might liken to a chamber of vaporized gasoline under extreme pressure, was induced? Given a tense, hungry audience, ingenuous and untutored in regard to most arts, and especially in regard to that new art of the novel, is it surprising that William Hill Brown's *The*

2. Harriet Beecher Stowe, *Oldtown Folks*, Boston, Houghton Mifflin and Co., 1897, p.438.

Power of Sympathy and Susanna Rowson's *Charlotte Temple*, taking their cues from the sentimental sensibility of Sterne's *Tristram Shandy* and from the. virtuous sentimentality of Richardson's *Pamela*, should provide in the last ten years of the eighteenth century the spark of combustion?

All the subsequent ranting and preaching against novels, the attempt to suppress them in the home, like much of the raging against comic books a little more than a century later, served only to provide free publicity, to sweeten the stolen grapes.

What the sentimental novelists went on providing for generations was little more than a spark to ignite emotions ready and waiting to flame, widely and furiously at least, if not very deeply, for sentimentalism as discussed here is the evoking, or the attempted evoking of emotions not genuinely warranted by the situation. This situation may be one in life to which certain responses are essentially false, or it may be one in art, any art, in which either poor craftsmanship, or the incapacity to feel or think deeply, may invalidate the emotions called upon. The reader, the hearer, the observer senses this impulsively, often with distress, in direct proportion to the extent of her or his development as reader, hearer, or observer.

In any discussion of the sentimental novels, it quickly becomes apparent that many of the ideas characteristic of them are also ideas frequently attributed to the romantic movement. The later sentimental novelists, for example, looked upon everyone as of good and benevolent instincts;[3] the

3. Herbert Ross Brown, *The Sentimental Novel in America, 1789-1860,*

Harriet Beecher Stowe:

romantics held man originally good but corrupted by society. The sentimentalists frequently set the stage with Gothic summer houses and strange gardens; the romantics were often addicted to the appeal of the distant, the exotic. The sentimentalists prettified death, corpses, and an imminent heaven; the romantics wrote of an eternal life both before and after "death" on earth. The list could be extended considerably, yet one should not fall into the error of assuming that the two movements, both of which had considerable influence on American literature, are the same thing. Craftsmanship, artistic purpose, depth and subtlety of feeling separate them, the romantics being superior on every count to their bargain-basement counterparts. The sentimental novelists are divorced from any realities concerning the individual's inner life, behavior, and society; the romantics are not. Yet no utterly sharp division exists. Some writers, parts even of the works of some writers, will rest on one side or the other of an uncertain shadow line.

E. Douglas Branch has provided a sharp and useful definition of the two attitudes:

> Romanticism I take to be three-pronged: the recognition of the reality; the passing of judgment upon it; and the clinging to the myth. Sentimentalism is the refusal to recognize the reality; or the inability to pass judgment upon it; and the clinging to the myth. It is the immature phase of the Romantic Movement.[4]

When, therefore, Branch wrote, "Mrs. Stowe tried, with *The Minister's Wooing*, to become a lady

Durham, N.C., Duke University Press, pp. 38 and 176.
4. E. Douglas Branch, *The Sentimental Years, 1836-1860*, New York, D. Appleton-Century Co., 1934, p. viii.

Woman and Artist

novelist, but she could not reach that particular eminence,"[5] he tossed, with his left hand, a light bouquet in the direction of the author of *Uncle Tom's Cabin*, for to be declared unable to qualify as a member in good standing of the "d----d mob of scribbling women" about whom Hawthorne complained is a compliment to one's talent and creative impulse.[6] To declare, at the same time, that a writer made an effort to join the league of the sentimental novelists, is a kind of rebuke, a criticism of good literary judgment, of craftsmanship, but one that can be aimed justly at no small number of writers of American fiction between 1800 and 1880.

Chita, heroine of James Fenimore Cooper's *The Wing-and-Wing*, converts the atheist hero to a belief in a hereafter only an hour or two before she closes his eyes and throws her body across his corpse, "and for a time there was danger that her own spirit might pass away in the paroxysm of her grief."[7] The characters in Cooper's *Afloat and Ashore* and *Miles Wallingford* are put through all the patterns of the sentimental appeal, including a heroine's leaving $20,000 to her lover-deceiver, a confirmed cliche of the sentimental novelists.[8]

Walt Whitman, greatly in need of money in 1842, wrote, "with the help of a bottle of port," a temperance novel that was thoroughly immersed in the sentimental tradition, a book that he himself later

5. E. Douglas Branch, pp. 131-132.
6. Caroline Ticknor, *Hawthorne and His Publisher*, Boston, Houghton Mifflin Co., 1913, p. 141.
7. James Fenimore Cooper, *The Wing-and-Wing*, New York, Belford, Clarke & Co., 1887, pp. 397-402.
8. H. R. Brown, p. 298.

called "damned rot—rot of the worst sort—."[9] *Franklin Evans, or The Inebriate*, in which a dying little girl drops a temperance tract into the palm of her alcoholic brother, thereby reforming him forever,[10] brought the author a hundred and twenty-five dollars.[11]

The tide of the sentimental novel in America which had begun to flood in the 1790s with the publication of *The Power of Sympathy* and with the first of a hundred and sixty-one known editions of *Charlotte Temple*, reached truly impressive proportions by the middle years of the nineteenth century. Herbert Ross Brown, in his book covering sentimental fiction over that period, lists more than one hundred writers, and of course an even greater number of titles, all influenced by, or propagating, or both, the tradition of quick and easy emotion from the printed page.

Hannah Webster Foster's *The Coquette*, perhaps the most readable of the early sentimental stories, appeared in at least one edition every year from 1797 to 1833,[12] and the books of Mary Jane Holmes, author of, among others, *Lena Rivers*, 1847, sold an estimated two million copies during her lifetime.[13] Isaac Mitchell's *Alonzo and Melissa*, 1811 (?), has been called "one of the most popular novels ever written in America;" it was so popular, in fact, that it was stolen by one Daniel Jackson, Jr. and published, over a long period of years, in an unrecorded number of editions.[14]   *The Lamplighter*, by Maria Suzanna

9. Walter Whitman, *Franklin Evans, or The Inebriate*, New York, Random House (Merrymount Press edition, Boston), 1929, p. xi.
10. Whitman, p. 165.
11. Whitman, p. vi.
12. B. M. Fullerton, *Selective Bibliography of American Literature, 1775-1900*, New York, William F. Payson, 1932, p. 105.
13. Fullerton, p. 143.
14. Fullerton, pp.196-197.

Cummins, sold 40,000 copies within eight weeks of publication date in 1854,[15] and Mrs. E.D.E.N. Southworth, author of *The Curse of Clifton,* 1853 (?), wrote twenty-nine highly popular books within twenty years,[16] and was responsible for sixty novels in all.[17] Lydia Maria Child, writer of *Hobomok* and other sentimental narratives, has been noted by bibliographer E.M. Fullerton thus:

> No American woman in her day and generation exerted a greater influence than Mrs. Child. . . .She shared with her [Mrs. Sedgewick] the honor of being the most succesful feminine writer of the early nineteenth century. Her influence as a molder of nationwide feminine opinion transcended the boundaries of her literary achievement.[18]

Seduction and sensibility were rampant in these works. A free-and-easy epistolary formlessness was almost as much a stock in trade as were moralizing, coincidents to prevent anything from coming out right, and soft idealization of easeful death. Worn situations and conventional characters were as customary as the lack of humor and the avowals that the book's material was based on fact.

Novels were written apparently only from the highest motives and were avowed exhortations to virtue. Whitman reprinted a portion of *Franklin Evans* in *The Brooklyn Eagle* and asked and answered his own question in the paper's editorial column:

> Can anyone say *The Brooklyn Eagle* is remiss in its duty, to use what influence it may have, in helping

---

15. Fullerton, p. 76.
16. Fullerton, p. 253.
17. Fred Lewis Pattee, *The Feminine Fifties*, New York, D. Appleton-Century Co., 1940, p. 122.

---

along this noble reform? We trow not. We consider temperance one of the grand regenerators of the age.[19]

The tradition of writing for the good of the readers was not new in the 1840s. In one of her prefaces, Mrs. Rowson declares:

> If the following tale should save one hapless fair one from the errors which ruined poor Charlotte, or rescue from impending misery the heart of one anxious parent, I shall feel a much higher gratification in reflecting on this trifling performance than could possibly result from the applause which might attend the most elegant, finished piece of literature whose tendency might deprave the heart or mislead the understanding.[20]

Chapters II, III, XXIX, XXX, of *The Power of Sympathy* were designed as long lectures from Mrs. Holmes to Myra on the dangers to young women of bad taste in reading and poor manners. The lectures were complete, even to a footnote equal to half a chapter. One letter in *The Coquette* held forth on Boston entertainment of the day. The stage was our _____ ? because tragedy was too gloomy. The circus was vulgar. Only a visit to the museum passed muster. These paragraphs marked the only pages in the book where the writer's attention wandered from the ethics of mating.[21]

The plots of the sentimental novels displayed a weakness for the accidents that by a hair prevented anything from coming out right, or, sometimes, wrong. Herbert Ross Brown has commented in regard to such

18. Fullerton, p. 50.
19. Whitman, p. vii.
20. Susanna Rowson, *Charlotte Temple*, New York, Funk & Wagnalls Co., 1905, p. 5.
21. Hannah Webster Foster, *The Coquette*, Boston, William Fetridge and Co., 1855, p. 197.

books that

> Should a distressed female wandering "from the
> desarts [sic] of Siberia" to England in quest of her
> husband happen to lose her way in the forests of
> Poland, a friendly light in the clearing was likely to be
> shining from the house of her brother. If the villain
> found it necessary to seek shelter in a miserable hovel
> during a storm, he was certain to be confronted by the
> corpse of the innocent fair he had previously seduced
> and harried to death.[22]

Not everyone was pleased with the cheap literary
output of the times. *Harper's Magazine* in 1855
published an anonymous parody of *The Lamplighter*[23]
and *The New York Herald* in 1848 inveighed against
much of the book trade with: "This species of literature
is actually unfit to read. . . . We venture to say that
there is not one of those authors who could write a
respectable, readable, pithy and sensible leading
editorial for a newspaper. . . ."[24]

And within a month of publication of Fanny
Fern's *Ruth Hall, Harper's Magazine* intoned in part:

> Here lies *Ruth Hall.* Has it a single great literary
> merit? Is there any story at all? Is there any
> individualization or development of character? Is there
> any sentiment which is not sentimentality of the worst
> kind? . . . Is there any pathos that is not puerile and
> factitious?[25]

Meade Minnigerode observed in 1924 that the
judgment of the editorial in *The New York Herald* has
been unimpeachable:

22. H. R. Brown, pp. 174-175.
23. Pattee, p. 112.
24. Meade Minnigerode, *The Fabulous Forties*, New York, G. F. Putnam's
Sons, 1924, pp. 105-106.
25. Pattee, p. 119.

Harriet Beecher Stowe:

They were reading an enormous amount of trash in America in the Forties. Sentimental, romantic, adventurous trash, staggering pompously on stilts through freshets of tears, much of it native and a great deal of it imported from England in paper covers.[26]

Two paragraphs from *Guilford, or Tried by His Peers*, may serve to dissolve any lingering doubts about the character of what may have been a literary nadir:

He could barely keep his legs; it had mustered all his faculties to pronounce what he had, and he had nearly failed at that; and then awful was the change that came upon his features. The little tuft upon his chin glowed in fire, his hair moved as if it had life. All the paleness, all the unnatural, deathly pallor, was gone. His eyes looked like two balls of blood and seemed shooting from their sockets. The bloody witnesses of the struggle within.

"Then Drysdale is my brother—the heir!" he repeated, and he fell back, never to rise again, clutching the air as he descended.[27]

Nor were novels all. Sentimentalism invaded not only the literary valleys of America during the middle decades of the nineteenth century, but in its cheaper incarnations it swept through architecture, painting, music, and lyrics, while gentility, shocked by the grossness of so many crude and lusty citizens, in overcompensation, besieged not only manners, but letters.

Paine and Burgess of New York published in 1846 *The Modern Builder's Guide*, including chapters on Applied Geometry and Practical Carpentry. The volume boasted ninety copper-plate engravings,

26. Minnigerode, p. 107.
27. Minnigerode, p. 108.

eighty-nine of which pictured a species of corrupt Greek architecture to which the builder might add such flourishes as suited his temper. Only the ninetieth plate displayed Gothic, a church. Already author-designer Minard LaFever was more than a decade behind the times; by 1830 Washington Irving "had his Tarrytown house completely coated with Gothic in the manner of baronial England."[28] William Strickland in the Thirties and Forties began indulging in curves, ornaments and cupolas, while

> Benjamin Latrobe, credited with having brought the Parthenon to America in his gripsack, carried the "Greek Revival" over the Alleghenies . . . even to Indiana and Illinois.
> You may call it romantic farce. The results appeared in the forms of banks and barns and tombs and churches of cities which boasted such names as Athens, Ithaca, Sparta, Syracuse, Rome, and Troy, which were bursting with templed porticoes. . . . Matters went from bad to worse. The Greek Revival became the Gothic Revival, or rather a hybrid revival in which cardboard Romanesque, Oriental, or Swiss models gave complicated flavor to Italian villas. . . . Men of banks or ships or coal paid money for these fantastic dreams of luxury while their wives egged them on into the furbelows of "Steamboat Gothic."[29]

Englishman Joseph Philip Knight, late in February, 1839, sang, at a benefit for the Indigent Female Assistance Society in New York, several of his most popular songs, including "Oh, Lord, I Have Wandered" and "The Veteran." Three days later he offered T. H. Bayly's "She Wore a Wreath of Roses," a

---

28. Homer Saint-Gaudens, *The American Artist and His Times*, New York, Dodd Mead and Co., 1941, p. 83.
29. Saint-Gaudens, pp. 63-64.

Harriet Beecher Stowe:

selection "in which the unfortunate heroine is introduced, first wearing roses, then orange blossoms, and finally a widow's sombre cap."[30]

The next year John Hill Hewitt wrote, and Henry Russell apparently appropriated, "The Old Arm Chair": "I love it! I love it, and who shall dare / To chide me for loving that old arm chair?" while T. H. Bayly scored success with "Oh, No, We Never Mention Her," and "She Never Blamed Him, Never."

> She sighed when he caress'd her
>   For she knew that they must part;
> She spoke not when he press'd her
>   To his young and panting heart;
> The banners waved around her
>   And she heard the bugles sound—
> They pass'd—and strangers found her
>   Cold and lifeless on the ground.[31]

It was a work to compete with "The Last Link Is Broken" for being the best example of 1840 noble resignation:

> The last link is broken
>   That bound me to thee
> And words I have spoken
>   Have rendered me free;
> That bright glance misleading
>   On others may shine,
> Those mild eyes unheeding
>   When tears burst from mine;
> If my love was deemed boldness
>   That error is o'er,
> I've witnessed thy coldness
>   And prize thee no more.

---

30. John Tucker Howard, *Our American Music*, New York, Thomas Y. Crowell, 1931, p. 169.
31. Howard, pp. 172-173.

Refrain
I have not loved thee lightly;
I'll think on thee yet;
I'll pray for thee nightly
Till life's sun has set.[32]

By 1847 Jasper Francis Cropsey Cole had already been three years hard at work painting landscapes in Connecticut, along the Hudson, at Lake George, and had completed "Greenwood Lake from Orange Country."[33] I. B. Woodbury wrote the words and music of "Be Kind of the Loved Ones at Home," and Charles T. White composed and wrote "De Floating Scow," also known as "Carry Me Back to Ole Virginny." The Mexican War was still being fretted out; New Hampshire legalized the ten-hour day; members of Colonel J.D. Stevenson's 7th Regiment of New York Volunteers staged minstrel shows in San Francisco at Leidesdorff's City Hotel; and following clashes over polygamy in Nauvoo, Illinois, a group of Latter Day Saints, under the leadership of Brigham Young, pushed westward into Utah to escape from the United States and establish Salt Lake City.[34] Two years later Worthington Whittredge, landscape artist, left Cincinnati to go to Paris where he would learn to paint better;[35] the well-dressed woman puffed her hair over a cushion atop her head; Stephen Foster wrote "Nelly Bly"; and gas light was installed in the White House.[36]

---

32. Howard, p. 183.
33. Eugen Neuhaus, *The History and Ideals of American Art*, Stanford, Cal., Stanford University Press, 1931, p. 74.
34. Julius Mattfield, compiler, *Variety Music Cavalcade*, New York, Prentice-Hall, 1952, pp. 72-73.
35. Neuhaus, p. 72.
36. Mattfield, p. 77.

Came the Fabulous Fifties, and Walter Hunt, who had already invented the safety pin, devised the paper collar; Alice Hawthorne, a pseudonym for Septimius Winner, wrote "What is Home Without a Mother?"; the Emigrant Aid Society sent two thousand anti-slavery New Englanders to settle in Kansas,[37] and American Gothic reached some species of eminence, crenellated turret-tops and all, with the building of The House of Mansions at Fifth Avenue and Forty-Second Street.[38] Crowding his canvasses with minute detail, John P. Kensett completed "Mount Washington From Conway," "The Hudson River From Fort Putnam," and "Sunset on the Adirondacks." Of the Hudson River School, Eugen Neuhaus later wrote:

> It is undoubtedly often timid, even niggled, in brushwork, and when it is least convincing it gives the impression of having been painted by spectacled pedants comfortably sitting on cushioned stools and painstakingly counting out, by means of a very small brush, every leaf on every tree, no matter how distant. their painstaking search for insignificant detail seems almost an obsession today. . . . We must remember, however, that through this microscopic study they sincerely hoped to express truth. . . .[39]

Writers of etiquette books, valiantly struggling to stem the tides of a vulgar and vigorous humanity, cautioned against "rinsing and gargling from finger bowls,[40] blowing the nose at the table, or even outdoors with the fingers,[41] and elbowing and pushing

37. Branch, picture opposite p. 160.
38. Neuhaus, pp. 66-67.
39. Dixon Wector, *The Saga of American Society*, New York, Charles Scribner's Sons, 1937, p. 165.
40. Minnigerode, p. 80.
41. Wector, p. 168.

for the best seats at stemaboat tables. The waltz was too intimate a dance for any but a married woman to indulge in, and then only at private homes with her and her husband's closer friends. If a lady chose to ensconce herself on the ground, her escort was not properly at liberty to follow her example unless she specifically invited him to be seated."[42]

Homer Saint-Gaudens wrote of the times:

> . . .the "America" won its sailing race around the Isle of Wight, and Queen Victoria was informed that "there was no second." Harvard put overboard its shell, to go rowing with Yale. Rifle shooting for turkey prizes proved the main attraction at county fairs. Fox hunting developed the enthusiasm of the dandies. The rowdies bet on cockfights. Skating in Central Park furnished gaiety for the Knickerbockers. Of a fall, cornhusking bees combined pleasure with practical results for the homely. The newly-minted millionaires . . . vacationed at Saratoga and drove their trotting horses down the speedway. The religious held camp meetings in shady groves. Travelers put their boots on George Pullman's plush cushions and snapped their embroidered suspenders.[43]

Franklin Pierce, fifth in the list of six consecutive undistinguished presidents, won the election of 1852, after Major Jack Downing had reputedly gone out of his way, returning from the Baltimore convention to Downingville, Maine, to visit Concord, New Hampshire, and discover whether General Pierce was a real person. He was, too. The neighbors knew him. Called into action at Chapultepec, the General had fainted, fallen from his horse and wounded his own leg.[44]

---

42. Saint-Gaudens, p. 87.
43. Branch, pp. 25-26.
44. Branch, pp. 25-26.

And in Boston a leading publisher rejected a novel authored by a little-known short-story writer, the wife of a Bowdoin College professor at Brunswick, Maine, one of the heaviest rejection mistakes, in a financial sense, ever made. The editor feared that publishing *Uncle Tom's Cabin* might injure his firm's trade with the South.[45]

45. Pattee, p. 132.

II. THE SENTIMENTAL PATTERN

Did Harriet Beecher read the sentimental novelists? If she did, no biographer has unearthed a record of it, yet the sentimental novelists' devices occur with impressive frequency throughout her books.

The Beecher family at the time of Harriet's childhood frowned upon all but a very few writers of fiction, and the exceptions were not the sentimentalists. Elder sister Catherine, who exerted a powerful influence over the adolescent Harriet, had in the 1820s strong and uncomplimentary opinions regarding the lady novelists of her day.[1] Harriet enjoyed at first a small room of her own while she was attending Catherine Beecher's Hartford Female Seminary, and apparently gained enough privacy to write no small part of a poetic drama about a young, noble, and finally converted profligate in Ancient Rome, before sister Catherine caught her at it. Where she had privacy to write, she had also, of course, privacy to read.

Lyman Beecher by then had moved to Boston, and Edward Beecher reported that, at home on vacations, Harriet consumed every book she could

1. Catherine Gilbertson, *Harriet Beecher Stowe*, New York, D. Appleton-Century Co., 1937, pp. 66-67.

reach.[2] She did read at some time *Sir Charles Grandison* by Samuel Richardson, who was to no small extent the root and source of more than a century of sentimental books.. It seems unlikely that she could totally have escaped sampling the works of Susanna Rowson, Lydia Maria Child, Catherine Sedgwick, or some of their kind, especially after the Beecher clan had migrated to Cincinnati, in 1832, where, owing to her age, Harriet enjoyed greater independence. Doubtless she scorned and disliked much of their work if she read it as a grown woman. Years later, in *Pink and White Tyranny*, she had unkind things to say about sentimentalists as she envisioned them:

> Charlie Ferrola was one of those whose softness and pitifulness, like that of sentimentalists generally, was only one form of intense selfishness. The sight of suffering pained him, and his first impulse was to get out of the way of it.[3]

As she portrayed Ferrola, he used every sad or tragic occasion for self-indulgence in grief, making himself the center of attention. Herbert Ross Brown later seconded her opinion about sentimental characters of this stripe: "The impulses which prompted self-abnegation were rarely free from the taint of exhibitionism and of a selfish indulgence in the feelings."[4] Mrs. Stowe also labelled the sentimental mind as one "that might not be unaptly represented by a bale of cotton,—downy, soft, benevolently fuzzy, and

---

2. Charles H. Foster, *The Rungless Ladder*, Durham, N.C., Duke University Press, 1954, p. 14.
3. Harriet Beecher Stowe, *Pink and White Tyranny*, Boston, Houghton Mifflin Co, 1918, p. 487.
4. H. R. Brown, p. 299.

---

confused."[5]

She never, of course, thought of herself as a sentimental novelist. What sincere writer does? To oneself, everyone is reporting the actual, or probing for the truth, or both, and in this unguarded state it is easy to fall prey to the very faults a writer scorns in others. The writer, of necessity also a reader, is ever in danger of following literature at the moment when she or he should be observing life.

Whether an influence stems from book A or B or C is perhaps unimportant, for the spirit of an age, so far as one can discover it, is expressed as effectively in manners, in speech, in casual songs, in design, as in popular fiction, and it is only the very strong who fully escape the great provincialisms of fashion and of time. Mrs. Stowe, sharp critic that she was in many respects, was not one of these. The sentimental sprout did not bud on every page, but, hardy perennial that it was, it blossomed in some form in all her novels.

She was never addicted, for instance, to the seduction story as the chief theme and backbone of a novel, yet in some of her books seduction, or the threat thereof, figures largely, and the treatment often produces a tone readily familiar to the reader of sentimental romances. Strangely enough, *Oldtown Folks*, frequently and justly praised for its picture of colonial, rural New England life, includes her most extensive use of seduction for plot complication. Alone in this book of Mrs. Stowe's does the seduction actually take place. In her other novels seducers generally fail, except for some of the slave owners who, of course, own women as chattels.

5. H. R. Brown, p. 279.

In the final chapters of *Oldtown Folks*, following a great deal of more important material, Tina, bride of the handsome, intelligent Ellery Davenport, twenty years her senior, is faced on her wedding night by one Emily Rossiter. Emily is the husband's noble-minded and now discarded mistress, who years ago ran away to Europe. Now she comes back with her child and declares herself to Tina because she believes no marriage should begin on a basis of falsehood. Tina's response a day or two later is to settle some of her own money on Emily, to reconcile the Puritan Rossiter family to their erring sister (a rather considerable accomplishment) and to adopt and love the child.

Sensational as this is when put in a few words, it remains a cut above many of the sentimental seductions of the century. Nobody dies, in childbirth or otherwise, with saccharine words of forgiveness and repentance on her lips, and Tina's final reactions to the revelation are refreshingly practical. Yet when the reader approaches the passages that tell of Emily's departure for Europe, and of the conventional responses of her brother, and others, to her return, the seduction-cliché flavor becomes apparent:

> She left ostensibly to go on a visit to Boston to her aunt, and all that was ever heard from her after that was a letter of final farewell to Miss Mehitable, in which she told her briefly, that, unable any longer to endure the life she had been leading, she had chosen her lot for herself, and requested her neither to seek her out nor to inquire after her, as all such inquiries would be absolutely in vain.[6]

Near the conclusion of the book, when Emily's

---

6. H. B. Stowe, *Oldtown Folks*, p. 390.

---

story unfolds, the narrator, Horace Holyoke, reports:

> The color flashed into Mrs. Rossiter's cheeks, and he suddenly leaned forward over the papers and covered his face with his hands. . . .
> "Horace," said Miss Mehitable, "the thing we feared has come upon us. O Horace, Horace! why could we not have known it in time?"

Five paragraphs later Mr. Rossiter says:

> "I would sooner have seen Tina in her grave than married to such a man," . . .
> "Oh Harry!" said Miss Mehitable.
> "I would!" he said, rising excitedly. "There are things that men can do that still leave hope of them; but a thing like this is *final*—it is decisive."[7]

The would-be seducer of *The Minister's Wooing* is Aaron Burr. Suave, likable, courteous, . . . and far from trustworthy, endowed with the intellect of a Puritan but with none of the piety, Burr apparently served as model for Ellery Davenport in *Oldtown Folks*, which was written a decade later. So similar are the two men as she delineates their characters that for a reader of both books they seem to be the same person, even to being grandsons of Jonathan Edwards.

Burr's campaign, which is of no importance to the main theme of the novel and could easily be omitted, is aimed at Mme. de Frontignac, a young French woman with an older husband. To display the workings of Burr's mind, Mrs. Stowe resorts to the well-worn device of displaying the seducer's letters written to a distant friend, a manoeuvre reminiscent of *The Coquette*:

---

7. H. B. Stowe, *Oldtown Folks*, p. 585.

I saw the prettiest little Puritan there (at the Wilcoxes' wedding party) that I have set eyes on for many a day. I really couldn't help getting up a flirtation with her, although it was much like flirting with a small copy of the "Assembly Catechism,"—of which last I had enough years ago, Heaven knows.[8]

A somewhat diluted descendent of Burr's and Davenport's is Harry Endicott of *Pink and White Tyranny*. Endicott has been rejected in the past by the now married Lillie, solely because he was not rich. His purpose, now that he has money, is not to seduce Lillie, but to make her suffer jealousy. As the action unrolls, however, toward the point at which not Harry, but Lillie, makes the illicit overture, the reader senses a certain familiarity in the tone of the writing, and feels a certainty that he is back at least on the edge of the sentimental stencil where, again as in *The Coquette*, man seduces by way of revenge.

The fact was that Harry Endicott hated Lillie now, with that kind of hatred which is love turned wrong side out. he hated her for the misery she had caused him and was in some danger of feeling it incumbent on himself to go to the devil in a wholly unnecessary manner on that account.[9]

Of the unmarried girl that Harry Endicott is courting in order to torment Lillie the author writes:

Rose walked through all her part in this little drama wrapped in a veil of sacred ignorance. Had she known the whole, the probability is that she would have refused Harry's acquaintance; but like many

---

8. Harriet Beecher Stowe, *The Minister's Wooing*, New York, Derby & Jackson, 1859, p. 234.
9. H. B. Stowe, *Pink and White Tyranny*, p. 153.

another nice girl, she tripped gayly near to pitfalls and chasms of which she had not the remotest conception.[10]

By the time Mrs. Stowe wrote *We and Our Neighbors*, published in 1875, she was prepared to relegate seduction not only to a subsidiary plot but to a minor character, and to sketch in the seduction itself in a single paragraph. Maggie's past in New York is quickly told:

> This poor Maggie had the misfortune to be very handsome. She was so pretty as a little girl, her mother tells me, as to attract constant attention; and I rather infer that the father and mother both made a pet and plaything of her, and were unboundedly indulgent. The girl grew up handsome, and thoughtless, and self-confident, and so fell an easy prey to a villain who got her to leave her home, on a promise of marriage which he never kept. She lived with him a while in one place and another, and he became tired of her and contrived to place her in a house of evil, where she was entrapped and enslaved for a long time.[11]

Her seducer never even gets into the story, but Maggie appears in several chapters, giving the writer a chance to lecture her readers on tolerance of and mercy for the fallen. They are very proper lectures, but their only effect on the art of fiction is to help spoil it.

Mrs. Stowe wrote no epistolary novels. Indeed, that fashion, which the early sentimentalists apparently took from Samuel Richardson to serve their own ends, had lost its wide popularity among writers long before 1850. Still its influence is clearly present in

10. H. B. Stowe, *Pink and White Tyranny*, p. 465.
11. Harriet Beecher Stowe, *We and Our Neighbors*, Boston, D. Lothrop & Co., 1875, p. 229.

all but one or two of Mrs. Stowe's longer works of fiction, and she often uses it as the sentimental writer's device.

No book, of course, may be justly labelled sentimental simply because it includes one or more letters. What the sentimental novelists did was over-use and abuse the epistolary form, permitting the letters to flaunt stilted diction, cloak moral lectures, repeat action already adequately covered, as in the letter on page 212 of *Oldtown Folks*, and to substitute rather sloppily for straight dramatic or narrative writing. Chapter XLI of *My Wife and I* offers an example of this kind of writing. The mass of petty and inconsequential detail that fails to further anything in atmosphere, in character, or in action, is exceedingly oppressive.

Mrs. Stowe was elsewhere sometimes guilty of these offenses. She had a weakness for lecture-sermons, and letters presented her with an ideal opportunity for indulgence in them. George Harris, of *Uncle Tom's Cabin*, writes four printed pages to a friend on the subject of American Negroes' colonizing of Liberia.[12] In *Dred*, Harry Gordon, from the depths of a southern swamp, pens an excellent three pages on American History, the rights of man, and the Bible as a Mulatto slave sees them.[13] Mary Scudder, of *The Minister's Wooing*, writes a four-page letter to the Calvinist, Dr. Hopkins, although he is boarding in the same house with her, concerning her love of God and her inability to feel alienated from Him.[14]

---

12. Harriet Beecher Stowe, *Uncle Tom's Cabin*, Boston, Houghton Mifflin and Co., 1892, vol. ii, pp. 357-361.
13. Harriet Beecher Stowe, *Dred, A Tale of the Great Dismal Swamp*, Boston, Phillips, Sampson and Co., 1856, vol. ii, pp. 201-203.
14. H. B. Stowe, *The Minister's Wooing*, pp. 291-294.

Letters in *My Wife and I,* and *We and Our Neighbors* (the first with forty-five and the second with sixty pages of epistolary form) discuss such topics as marriage, the place of woman in society and in the home, religious forms, fashions, house-hunting, housekeeping, cooking, and the conduct of social life.[15] Mrs. Stowe began *My Wife and I* in the first person through narrator Harry Henderson. For many chapters Henderson is not very close to his fiancée-to-be, so to show the thought and character of her heroine, Mrs. Stowe casually inserts entire chapters of the letters of Eva Van Arsdel to one friend or another, and sometimes the chatty replies. Harry Henderson never mentions these letters and apparently does not know of them. They often cover parts of the story already narrated and sometimes add nothing. At other points they do advance the book but are not one whit more useful for that purpose than straight narrative would be. When she wrote *We and Our Neighbors,* a continuation of *My Wife and I,* Mrs. Stowe gave up the narrator and wrote in the third person, but clung to and even expanded the use of letters.

The Pearl of Orr's Island includes one letter twenty pages long which has a second letter buried within it.[16] The letter is never mailed; it is simply handed from the writer to the intended reader, who takes it away and reads it. The chapter is flashback material which could have been handled as well, perhaps better, through straight narrative, or even extended dialogue.

15. Harriet Beecher Stowe, *My Wife and I,* Boston, D. Lothrop & Co., 1871: pp. 176-178, 210-215, 435-438, 441-443, 446-447; and *We and Our Neighbors,* pp. 23-29, 42-51, 227-231, 290-306.
16. Harriet Beecher Stowe, *The Pearl of Orr's Island,* Cambridge, The Riverside Press, 1896, pp. 245-265.

Jonathan Rossiter's letters in *Oldtown Folks* are clear, witty, and include some of the best passages in the book, but too often their contribution is one toward social documentation rather than to the art of fiction. Letters from Dolly Cushing to her parents, constituting the final chapters of *Poganuc People*, are in a sense unnecessary. Dolly visits Boston, swerves toward, if not into the Episcopal Church, and meets the young man to whom she will become engaged. The reader does not see the parents react to her letters, does not read their replies, does not even know that they made any. Seven-eighths of the book has been told in the third person, and the omniscient author could go to Boston with Dolly to detail the scene, except perhaps that she was in a hurry to finish her last book, and letters were ever the hurried writer's friend.

A perusal of Mrs. Stowe's books will soon make clear that she shrank from writing the scene of sexual passion, even though it were legal and proper. Again and again she bridled, put aside her pen, or turned the page, as in *The Pearl of Orr's Island, Dred,* and *Poganuc People.* This may have been a revulsion on her part from the fulsome love scenes that had already been and were still being perpetrated by others, or it may have been merely the product of inhibition in this particular Puritan-bred, Victorian gentlewoman, or both. If she could not do them well, we should thank her for not trying. There are worse things in an artist than restraint. What she did do was resort to letters for a report of courtship and love scenes, especially in *My Wife and I, We and Our Neighbors,* and *Poganuc People*—late books all. This technique kept the embarrassing moment at one remove from both author and reader. It also weakened the story and materially increased the number of letters in her novels.

In fairness it should be stated that no letters at all mark the pages of *Agnes of Sorrento* and that some of Mrs. Stowe's letters are legitimate off-stage messengers.[17] Others sometimes serve to delineate the characters of the letter-writers, even as did a few in *The Coquette*,[18] but more often they are evidence of the casual writing habits to which she and many others were addicted.

Doubtless Harriet Beecher Stowe's penchant for the beautiful and idealized death, especially of women and children, constitutes her strongest tie to the school of sentimental novelists. Charlotte Temple's death in her father's arms apparently impressed thousands of readers as a highly moving scene, but it is the passing of Eliza Wharton, of *The Coquette* that seems one of the more likely antecedents of Mrs. Stowe's dying women. "'I welcome Death as the angel of peace,'" Eliza says. "She uttered these words with a placid smile of resignation—her head sunk down on the pillow—and the next minute she was an angel."[19]

The death of Sue Cripps in Mrs. Stowes' *Dred* reads:

> "Tiff," she gasped, speaking with difficulty, "I've seen the one that said that, and it's all true, too! and I've seen all why I've suffered so much. He-He-He is going to take me! Tell the children about Him!" There was a fluttering sign, a slight shiver, and the lids fell over the eyes forever.[20]

---

17. H. B. Stowe, *Oldtown Folks*, p. 329.
18. H. B. Stowe, *The Minister's Wooing*, pp. 233-234.
19. H. W. Foster, *The Coquette*, p. 231.
20. H. B. Stowe, *Dred*, vol. i, p. 118.

Mara, of *The Pearl of Orr's Island* (a book in which six death and burials are recounted in the first seventy-one pages) says in her last days: "It is not so very terrible, if one would only think so, to cross that river. All looks so bright to me now that I have forgotten how sorrow seemed."[21]

Later the author reports:

> There came a day when the room so sacredly cheerful was hushed to a breathless stillness; the bed was then all snowy white, and that soft still sealed face, the parted waves of golden hair, the little hands folded over the white robe, all had a sacred and wonderful calm, a rapture of repose that seemed to say "it is done."[22]

Treatment of the death of Mrs. Higgins in *Poganuc People* is one of the rare exceptions in Mrs. Stowe's novels, one that will be discussed later, but the familiar tone is struck just a few paragraphs before the character's decease:

> "My dear husband," she said, "you know I love you."
> "Yes-yes, and you are the only one that does."
> "You needn't give me up; you must come with me. I want you to come where I am; I shall wait for you; you're an old man—it won't be long. . . ."[23]

As was not infrequently her habit, Mrs. Stowe here wrote of the beauty and peace of the corpse, of "rapturous repose," of a "mysterious smile," of "eyes gazing on an ineffable vision of bliss." Harry Henderson, of *My Wife and I*, loses his first beloved

---

21. H. B. Stowe, *Dred*, vol. ii, p. 137.
22. H. B. Stowe, *The Pearl of Orr's Island*, p. 388.
23. H. B. Stowe, *The Pearl of Orr's Island*, p. 395.

---

when both of them are about five. Mercifully he is himself sick and hence not present at the death, but Daisy appears to him later in a dream.

> "Didn't I tell you we'd see each other again?"
> "But they told me you were dead," I said in wonder.
> "I am not dead, dear Hazzy," she said. "We never die where I am—I shall love you always," and with that my dream wavered and grew misty as when clear water breaks an image into a thousand glassy rings and fragments.[24]

The narrator, a convenient alter ego for Mrs. Stowe, and as usual with her, a man, comments regarding this bereavement:

> It seems to be that lovely and loving childhood, with its truthfulness, its frank sincerity, its pure, simple love, is so sweet and holy an estate that it would be a beautiful thing in heaven to have a band of heavenly children, guileless, gay, and forever joyous—tender spring blossoms of the Kingdom of Light.[25]

Where, one wonders, was the Mrs. Stowe who had borne seven children and raised six, who was one of a family of eleven, and seemed to have quite a sharp memory of her own childhood, when she penned these half-truths? Consciously or otherwise, she may have been listening to the voice of literary fashion at the moment rather than regarding considered experience.

In Mrs. Stowe's novels men sometimes die without much affecting demonstration. The deaths of Ellery Davenport and Aaron Burr are merely reported

---

24. Harriet Beecher Stowe, *Poganuc People*, Boston, Houghton Mifflin Co., 1913, p. 203.
25. H. B. Stowe, *My Wife and I*, pp. 29-30.

---

to the reader, but Augustine St. Clare, of *Uncle Tom's Cabin*, dies in the more customary manner:

> "His mind is wandering," said the doctor.
> "No! it is coming HOME, at last! at last!" said St. Clare, energetically; "at last! at last!"
> They saw that the mighty hand was on him. Just before the spirit parted, he opened his eyes, with a sudden light, as of joy and recognition, and said, "Mother!" and then he was gone!"[26]

Little Eva's death, so often spoken of, and so many times transposed into even more gaudy scenes on the stage, is not very different from those already cited: "A bright, glorious smile passed over her face, and she said brokenly,—'Oh! love,—joy,—peace!' gave one sigh, and passed from death unto life!"[27]

No extensive comment should be required to underline the connection of this scene with the sentimental tradition.

Mrs. Stowe had two avowed reasons for writing *Dred, A Tale of the Great Dismal Swamp.* She wanted to place her story in the South where "there is no ground, ancient or modern, whose vivid lights, gloomy shadows, and grotesque groupings afford to the novelist so wide a scope for the exercise of his powers." Here was a setting which could "carry us back to the twilight of the feudal ages." She desired, in other words, something at least mildly Gothic, just as she did later when she wrote *Agnes of Sorrento* and set the scene in Italy at the time of Savonarola. Her second reason, which she considered "higher," was moral. It was necessary to provide another effective sermon on

---

26. H. B. Stowe, *My Wife and I*, p. 31.
27. H. B. Stowe, *Uncle Tom's Cabin*, v. ii, p. 182.

Woman and Artist

slavery.[28]

Few would quarrel today with Mrs. Stowe about her moral position regarding slavery. The point is, not that she was on the side of the angels, but that she assumed the moral dissertation belonged in the work of art. This idea, as well as the Gothic atmosphere, are both direct from the leaves of the sentimental novelists. That the sentimental novelists generally were at least ostensibly in the business of promoting virtue has been discussed in Chapter I. Any consideration of Mrs. Stowe's work must repeatedly consider the essays or lectures that she inserted everywhere. They have been mentioned already in connection with her use of letters, and will be considered again under other headings.

The sentimentalists' fondness for Gothic architecture, of a kind, and a semi-Gothic atmosphere not infrequently was expressed in the description of a wild kind of garden and of summer houses, such as the two in C. B. Brown's *Wieland.* Discussing the purpose and nature of these gardens and isolated porticoes in sentimental novels, Herbert Ross Brown reports that

> the landscape which art thus helped to cultivate for genteel females was designed to feed their melancholy and their love of solitary contemplation "in the bosom of nature." . . . The sentimental retreat was a favorite stage property. . . . The architectural style of these structures was a romantic hybrid of the Classical, Oriental, and Gothic.[29]

Examples of Gothic, except for *Agnes of Sorrento*, are not noticeably frequent in Mrs. Stowe's

---

28. H. B. Stowe, *Uncle Tom's Cabin*, v. ii, p. 149.
29. H. B. Stowe, *Dred*, v. i, p. iii.

---

work. She was right, however, about *Dred*; its dismal and, for the runaway slave, secure swamps have all the impenetrability, the shadows, the threatening quality she was searching for. Occasionally her Gothic reaches even into the bright sunlight of summer New England, at least in architecture.

> Here, embowered in blossoming trees, stood a little Gothic cottage, a perfect gem of rural irregularity and fanciful beauty. . . . From the porch a rustic bridge led across a little ravine into a summerhouse, which was built like a nest into the branches of a great oak which grew up from the hollow below the knoll.[30]

Even in *Poganuc People* Gothic briefly raises its mysterious arches, but only in the design of the small Episcopal chapel.[31] *Agnes of Sorrento* affords the best opportunity for this kind of scenery and properties, and accordingly provides capes, swords, castles, confederates in the city crowds, torchlight violence in a monastery, and a brisk rescue of the heroine from the clutches of lascivious powers in Rome.

One of the characteristic devices of the sentimental novelists also often employed by Mrs. Stowe is the convenient accident, or the coincidental meeting, for either good or ill, generally of related persons so long separated that they may be unknown to each other.

Thirty pages from the close of *Uncle Tom's Cabin*, one Mme. de Thoux, travelling on a Mississippi River boat, reveals in conversation with George Shelby that George Harris is her long unseen brother. A slave woman, Cassy, also on board, who has escaped with

---

30. H. R. Brown, pp. 134, 135.
31. H. B. Stowe, *Dred*, v. ii, p. 335.

Woman and Artist

Emmeline from Simon Legree's plantation, where Shelby has been lately hunting for Uncle Tom—Cassy discovers that Eliza Harris is her daughter.[32] Before this, Miss Ophelia's letter to the Shelbys, an effort to rescue Uncle Tom from the harshness of slave life in the deep South, has been unaccountably delayed en route.

Four pages from the end of *Dred*, a six-hundred-and-sixty-page novel, one read:

> Anne Clayton, on a visit to a friend's family in New Hampshire, met with Livy Ray, of whom she had heard Nina speak so much, and very naturally the two ladies fell into the most intimate friendship; visits were exchanged between them, and Clayton, on first introduction, discovered the lady he had met in the prison in Alexandria.[33]

Chapter VII of *The Pearl of Orr's Island* tells of the body of a woman, and her still-living baby, being washed ashore on a Maine coast island. Later the reader learns that the woman was a Spanish emigrée to Florida who years ago was beloved of her Yankee tutor. The tutor, by now the Rev. Mr. Sewall of Brunswick, Maine, is asked to come to the island to preach a funeral sermon for the unknown victim, and of course recognizes her in her coffin.

Near the conclusion of *The Minister's Wooing*, Miss Prissy, the dressmaker, in a postscript to a letter, writes:

> I forgot to tell you that Jim Marvyn has come home quite rich. He fell in with a man in China who was at the head of one of their great merchant-houses, whom

32. H. B. Stowe, *Poganuc People*, p. 17.
33. H. B. Stowe, *Uncle Tom's Cabin*, v. ii, pp. 347-350.

he nursed through a long fever, and took care of his business, and so, when he got well nothing would do but he must have him for a partner; and now he is going to live in this country and attend to the business of the house here.[34]

Ellery Davenport first meets the young people of *Oldtown Folks* while, as children, they are visiting in Boston. Twelve years later he marries the grown child, Tina, and it then develops that Emily Rossiter, more or less the mystery woman of village history, and sister to the woman who adopted Tina, has been these many years his mistress in Europe.

Bolton, the serious New York editor with whom Harry Henderson works, in *My Wife and I*, turns out to have taught school in Harry's New Hampshire home town while Harry was away at college, and to have been a suitor of Harry's cousin Caroline there, but Harry has known noting of all this.

The peasant heroine of *Agnes of Sorrento* makes a pilgrimage to Rome where quite by accident, during the final chapters, she comes to the attention of a woman who turns out to be her aunt on her lost father's side.

> "My Lord," said the Princess, "I see in this event the wonderful working of the good God. I have but just learned that this young person is my near kinswoman; it was only this morning that the fact was certified to me on the dying confession of a holy Capuchin, who privately united by brother to her mother."[35]

These, like nearly all the examples of Mrs. Stowe's indulgence in the sentimental, are the

---

34. H. B. Stowe, *Dred*, v. ii, p. 332.
35. H. B. Stowe, *The Minister's Wooing*, pp. 564-565.

---

employment of some particular and well-worn techniques of narration, of choice of background, of description, or of word choice in dialogue. Yet even all these elements, sprinkled here and there throughout a novel, do not provide it with the truly lush, amorphous, and saccharine atmosphere that exudes from the pages of a full-blown sentimental work. It is, precisely, the tone of sentimentalism that she lacks. Her lapses are tricks of the trade, bad habits she picked up from her, in a literary sense, low-brow contemporaries and predecessors. They do not rise from the inner folds of her artist's sense; if they did, they would be ever-present, and an overgenerous effulgence of adjectives would mar every page.

Mrs. Stowe was capable of writing with fairness and understanding of people whose opinions she did not share, even of people of whom she did not approve. She found humor a blessing, and unsavory facts also—some that, as an artist, she could not ignore. These are not the characteristics of a completely sentimental writer.

When one has said all this, however, the fact remains that she did exploit the sentimentalists' means, and although a few such links with the tear-stained handkerchief tradition would be of little significance, their continual reappearance makes it futile to deny that she was, in some ways, one of the sentimental novelists of her time. Unlike many lesser writers, however, she was much more besides, and the impressive fact about her may be that she was able to rise above the contemporary cloud as far as she did.

III. A SENSE OF REALISM

It is quite possible to read several of the sentimental novelists and wonder afterwards if any of these writers had seen anything in life as they lived it. Sometimes one imagines that the only thing that ever impressed them was the reading of other books, and not the best of other books either. No one need harbor such thoughts while reading the works of Harriet Beecher Stowe; she saw with her eyes; she heard with the ear; often she remembered and understood. Happily at times she was able to reproduce the speech, the vision, in a manner to convince the reader of her truth.

To mention a sense of realism at all is to invite ambiguity, for the word has too many casual and inexact meanings. Frequently it is interpreted as indicating the disagreeable, or sexual, or scatological, or even cynical, as if the disagreeable, or sexual, or scatological could not be idealized or sentimentalized, and as if a cynical representation were not an idealized one turned inside out. Realism, in this work, is representation without idealization. It is not necessarily ugly, or sordid, or neutral, or beautiful, but may be any of them within the limits of the definition. To say that realism is representation of life as it is, is meaningless. Who knows what it is? We may say, however, that it is representation of life on and below the surface, as a perceptive and conscientious observer has seen it, without idealization. How it will be judged will depend, in part, on the perception, memory, and honesty of the reader. This is a lugubrious and unhappy circumstance for an author, but it presents a hazard all writers must take.

When Mrs. Stowe in the following passage writes of trees that "dipped and rippled in the waters," she is undoubtedly speaking of the reflections of trees, which do exactly that along shore on a nearly calm, clear day such as she describes:

> . . . the sombre spruces and shaggy hemlocks that dipped and rippled in the waters were penetrated to their deepest recesses with the clear brilliancy of the sky—a true northern sky, without a cloud, without even a softening haze, defining every outline, revealing every minute point, cutting with sharp decision the form of every promontory and rock, and distant island.
>
> . . .
>
> Eagle Island lay on the blue sea, a tangled thicket of evergreens—white pine, spruce, arbor vitae, and fragrant silver firs.[1]

Many novelists have managed excellent descriptions in the century since Mrs. Stowe wrote, and it is difficult now, sometimes, to remember that at the time she composed hers they could stand out. One has only to compare them to less worthy parts of her own books, or to contemporary works by literary inferiors to appreciate her occasional touches. *Uncle Tom's Cabin* includes this:

In the bar-room he found assembled quite a

---

1. H. B. Stowe, *The Pearl of Orr's Island,* p. 160.

---

miscellaneous company, whom stress of weather had driven to harbor, and the place presented the usual scenery of such reunions. Great, tall, raw-boned Kentuckians, attired in hunting-shirts, and trailing their loose joints over a vast extent of territory, with the easy lounge peculiar to the race-rifles stacked away in the corner, shot-pouches, gamebags, hunting-dogs and little negroes, all rolled together in the corner—were the characteristic features in the picture.[2]

Some of Mrs. Stowe's best realistic writing graces the pages of her New England stories. The picture of the minister's woods, either the one in *Poganuc People* or *Oldtown Folks*, stays long in the mind of the reader. The Oldtown scene reads:

> We had . . . one of those sharp, clear, sunny winter days, when the sleds squeak over the flinty snow and the little icicles tingle along on the glittering crust as they fall from the trees, and the breath of the slow-pacing oxen steams up like a rosy cloud in the morning sun, and then falls back condensed in little icicles on every hair.[3]

Generally the dialogue in her books is not to the taste of the late-twentieth-century reader. Too often it is heroic, or quaintly rural, either of the Southern or New England variety, twisted and contorted with misspellings and apostrophes. The only way to get along with it and absorb what is good is to suspend, willingly, disbelief. Here and there come exceptions. These lines, from a Yankee farmer, were misspelled in

2. H. B. Stowe, *Uncle Tom's Cabin*, v. i, p. 155.
3. H. B. Stowe, *Oldtown Folks*, pp. 478-479.

an attempt to indicate the accent, but they have the convincing rhythm, the right words, the right feeling, and if anyone thinks a Yankee farmer won't talk that long at a stretch, he should go find one and listen.

> "Wal, railly, ef the deacon hain't come down with his shagbark! Wal, wal, the revival has operated on him some, I guess. Last year the deacon sent a load that I'd ha' been ashamed to had in my back yard, an' I took the liberty o' tellin' him so. God, straight-grained shagbark. Wal, wal! I'll go out an' help him unload it. Ef that'ere holds out to the bottom, the deacon's done putty wal, an' I shall think grace *has* made some progress.[4]

Like the above, no small number of Mrs. Stowe's best realistic passages are the humorous ones, deriving their voltage from a contrast of the real and the ideal. Many years of Negro stage comics make today's reader wary of her humorous slaves, and one can only hope that she drew from them on her memories of Cincinnati, and not on that unfortunate form of entertainment, the minstrel show. Many of the lines of her Negro characters may not have been clichés when she wrote them; they have since become so.

No such difficulties obstruct the reader's appreciation of Jonathan Rossiter's report of a conversation in a New England village store:

> You know everybody's religious opinions are a matter of discussion in our neighborhood, and Ezekiel Scranton . . . enjoys the celebrity of being an atheist, and rather values himself on the distinction. It takes a man of courage, you know, to live without a God; and

---

4. H. B. Stowe, *Oldtown Folks*, p. 483.

Harriet Beecher Stowe:

> Ezekiel gave himself out as a plucky dog, and able to
> hold the parson at bay. . . . So he meets him the other
> day in the store.
>
> "How's this, Mr. Scranton? they tell me you're an
> atheist!"
>
> "Well, I guess I be, Parson," says Ezekiel,
> comfortably.
>
> "Well, Ezekiel, let's talk about this. You believe in
> your own existence, don't you?"
>
> "No, I don't."
>
> "What! Not believe in your own existence?"
>
> "No, I don't." Then, after a moment, "Tell you what,
> parson, I ain't a going to be twitched up by none o'
> your syllogisms.[5]

The above examples are drawn from pleasant portions of Mrs. Stowe's books, but she was well aware, as was any child brought up in a Puritan family, that the sunny hours were in no majority. She was no better able to deal with scenes of violence, however, than she was with scenes of sexual passion, and the times might not have permitted her to do so if she could. Uncle Tom is beaten to death, but we do not really see the blows, nor the welts. We do not hear the whips strike nor see the twitch of the body. Tom Loker in *Uncle Tom's Cabin* is shot, then pushed down a cliff. The body falls, but we do not hear a sound nor feel the crush against rock.

"The coarse, the low, the mean, the vulgar," she wrote in *Poganuc People*, "is ever thrusting itself before the higher and more delicate nature, and claiming, in virtue of its very brute strength, to be the true reality."[6] There spoke the housewife who was also mother and writer, and no matter how much she

---

5. H. B. Stowe, *Oldtown Folks*, p. 224.
6. H. B. Stowe, *Poganuc People*, p. 178.

---

talked about "the higher and more delicate nature," the artist in her sometimes obliged her to use what were, by her lights, the low, the vulgar. She wrote many sentimental death scenes, but note this concerning the death of Mrs. Higgins:

> But the excitement and energy which had sustained the sick woman thus far had been too much for her; a blood-vessel was suddenly ruptured, and her mouth filled with blood. She threw up her hands with a slight cry. Zeph rose and rushed to the door, calling the nurse.[7]

Reporting the death of old Prue, the drunken slave woman whose last child has been starved to death and who herself wishes to die, Mrs. Stowe does not try to write a scene, the result being that the unconscious artist produces matter-of-fact and successful writing: "`. . . Prue, she got drunk agin—and they had her down cellar—and thar they left her all day, I hearn 'em saying that the flies had got to her—and she's dead!'"[8]

Residents of New Orleans, after *Uncle Tom's Cabin* was printed, hastened to point out that New Orleans had no cellars, and with a high water table could not have them. All was true enough, but not so serious an artistic error as falsifying emotions and behavior. Inhumanity, whether it be in a New England cellar, a Georgia hogpen, or a Mississippi corn crib, is still the same horrifying inhumanity.

Early in *The Pearl of Orr's Island*, Mrs. Stowe shows what she can do with the unrelieved depiction of a corpse neither sentimentalized into horror, nor

---

7. H. B. Stowe, *Poganuc People*, p. 198.
8. H. B. Stowe, *Uncle Tom's Cabin*, v. ii, p. 27.

---

into beauty:

> He was lying in a full suit of broadcloth, with a white vest and smart blue necktie, fastened with a pin, in which was braided hair under a crystal. All his clothing, as well as his hair, was saturated with sea water, which trickled from time to time, and struck with a leaden and dropping sound into a sullen pool which lay under the table.[9]

It would be a mistake to assume that Erskine Caldwell was the first to write of the grimness of life for the poor whites of the South. Mrs. Stowe managed quite well during some of her journeys into realism:

> And so discoursing, the good man at length arrived before the door of a miserable, decaying log cabin, out of whose glassless windows dark emptiness looked, as out of the eyeholes of a skull. Two scared, cowering children disappeared round the corner as he approached. He kicked open the door and entered. Crouched on a pile of dirty straw, sat a miserable, haggard woman, with large wild eyes, sunken cheeks, dishevelled, matted hair, and long, lean hands, like bird's claws. At her skinny breast an emaciated infant was hanging, pushing, with his little skeleton hands, as if to force the nourishment which nature no longer gave; and two scared-looking children, with features wasted and pinched blue with famine, were clinging to her gown. The whole group huddled together, drawing as far as possible away from the newcomer, looked up with large, frightened eyes, like hunted animals.[10]

Here is part of her portrait of Abijah Skinflint's family. It is only fair to mention that Abijah, like Simon Legree, is a New Englander living in the South, one of those whose meanness might have led Mrs.

---

9. H. B. Stowe, *The Pearl of Orr's Island,* p. 6.
10. H. B. Stowe, *Uncle Tom's Cabin,* v. i, p. 230.

Stowe to sympathize with the Southerners for prefixing the name with the adjective *damn.*

> "I say, Dad, stop!" called Polly from the window. "If you don't, I'll make work for you, 'fore you come home; you see if I don't! Durned if I won't!"
>
> "Come along then, can't you? Next time we go anywhere, I'll shut you up over night to begin to dress!"
>
> Polly hastily squeezed her fat form into a red calico dress, and, seeking a gay summer shawl, with her bonnet in her hand, rushed to the wagon and mounted, the hooks of her dress successively exploding, and flying off as she stooped to get in.
>
> "Durned if I know what to do!" said she; "this yer old durned gear coat's all off my back!"
>
> "Gals is always fools!" said Abijah consolingly.
>
> "Stick in a pin, Polly," said her mother, in an easy, singsong drawl.
>
> "Durn you, old woman, every hook is off!" said the promising young lady.
>
> "Stick in more pins then," said the mamma; and the vehicle of Abijah passed onward.[11]

Completing her sketch of Mrs. Ben Dakin, North Carolina poor white, the author reports:

> She was greatly given to eating clay, cleaning her teeth with snuff, and singing Methodist hymns, and had a very sincere concern for Ben's salvation. The little woman sat resignedly on the morning we speak of, while a long-limbed, broad-shouldered child of two years, with bristly white hair, was pulling her by the ears and hair, and otherwise maltreating her, to make her get up to give him a piece of bread and molasses. . . .[12]

Her description of Zeph Higgins at his wife's

---

11. H. B. Stowe, *Dred,* v. i, p. 283.
12. H. B. Stowe, *Dred,* v. i, p. 285.

---

funeral is perhaps more thoroughly impressive because it follows immediately a passage in which she describes the corpse as having a "delicate, lily-like beauty," with "a mysterious smile," and "rapturous repose."

> Among the mourners at the head of the coffin sat Zeth, like some rugged gray rock—stony, calm, and still. He shed no tear, while his children wept and sobbed aloud; only when the coffin-lid was put on, a convulsive movement passed across his face. But it was momentary, and he took his place in the procession to walk to the grave in grim calmness.[13]

Granting the powerful force of gentility in her time, when many of her fellow writers would have employed even greater and more flowery circumlocutions simply to mention a pregnancy, Mrs. Stowe did quite well to indicate with comparative plain speaking that her society matron, Lillie, was trying to induce miscarriage.

> Yet as Lillie spoke, she knew, in her own slippery little heart, that the shadow of this awful cloud of maternity was resting over her; though she laced and danced, and bid defiance to every law of nature, with a blind and ignorant willfulness, not caring what consequences she might draw down on herself if only she might escape this.[14]

Mrs. Stowe did not limit her passages of realism, however, to surfaces alone. One of the refreshing things about her is that she thought, and that during the two decades she lived in Cincinnati, she had opportunity to absorb ideas from, and discuss ideas

13. H. B. Stowe, *Poganuc People*, p. 203.
14. H. B Stowe, *Pink and White Tyranny*, p. 449.

with, others. Augustine St. Clare, in *Uncle Tom's Cabin*, is probably her most vociferous spokesman on matters economic and social. Addressing that excellently drawn Vermonter, Aunt Ophelia, St. Clare asks her: if the South should rise up and emancipate its slaves, who would educate them and teach them to use freedom? The South, he announces, is too lazy to do that, too impractical.

> "They will have to go north, where labor is the fashion . . .; and tell me, is there enough Christian philanthropy among your Northern States to bear the process of their education. . . ? If we emancipate are you willing to educate? How many families in your town would take in a negro man and woman. . . ? We are the more obvious oppressors of the negro; but the unChristian prejudice of the North is an oppressor almost equally severe.[15]

Mrs. Stowe had learned certain lessons about society similar to that one, which later generations had to learn for themselves. She knew that an idealist would be tolerated so long as he merely talked, or instituted the most gentle of humanitarian reforms, but that the moment he touched pocketbooks at the source, thunder would strike. Norman Thomas in 1931, or any other year, was considerably easier for conservatives to tolerate than was Franklin D. Roosevelt in 1935. Judge Clayton, in *Dred*, instructs his son, who is really a very decent idealist, about the facts of life in their society:

> ". . . the system, though ruinous in the long run to communities, is immediately profitable to individuals . . ., is a source of political influence. . . . The holders of

15. H. B. Stowe, *Uncle Tom's Cabin*, v. i, p. 281.

slaves . . . are united against the spirit of the age by a common interest and danger, and the instinct of self-preservation is infallible. . . .

"As a matter of personal feeling, many . . . would rejoice in some of the humane changes . . . you propose; but any change endangers the perpetuity of the system. Therefore they'll resist you at the very outset, not because they would not, many of them, be glad to have justice done, but because . . . they cannot afford it."[16]

Nor is her eye less sharp, apparently, when she turns to a Connecticut town at the time of her childhood in the early nineteenth century, and writes:

. . . there were in the town of Poganuc two distinct circles of people, who mingled in public affairs as citizens and in church as communicants, but who rarely or never met on the same social plane. There was the *haute noblesse*—very affably disposed, and perfectly willing to condescend; and there was the proud democracy, prouder than the *noblesse*, who wouldn't be condescended to, and insisted on having their way and their say, on the literal, actual standpoint of the original equality of human beings.[17]

Her depiction of a village situation here is by no means completely dated in all New England towns even today, despite the crystalizing of society into lower-uppers, upper-middles, lower-lowers, and such.

Mrs. Stowe wrote numerous romances of the boy-gets-girl pattern, generally with her own variations, twists, and personal attitudes. In *Dred* and *The Pearl of Orr's Island* the hero does not marry the woman he starts out for because Heaven intervenes. Horace Holyoke, narrator of *Oldtown Folks*, is deprived

16. H. B. Stowe, *Dred*, v. ii, pp. 151-152.
17. H. B. Stowe, *Poganuc People*, pp. 83-84.

of his inamorata for a few years while she is married to the charming libertine, Ellery Davenport, and the reader knows this is just as well, since if she had not married Davenport, she would have dreamed about an idealization of him the rest of her life. *Pink and White Tyranny* is the story of an unsatisfactory marriage, but *Agnes of Sorrento, The Minister's Wooing, Poganuc People, My Wife and I,* and *We and Our Neighbors* offer the conventional happy ending, far as some of them may stray in other respects. Mrs. Stowe did not, however, dodge the fact that people frequently married one of the "wrong" persons. She was also (and this was unusual among writers of her time) insistent that her characters, when in love, were in love not with an actuality but with a projected ideal. Jung's *anima-animus* would have seemed credible to her.

> In a refined and exalted nature, it is very seldom that the feeling of love, when once thoroughly aroused, bears any sort of relation to the reality of the object. It is commonly an enkindling of the whole power of the soul's love for whatever she considers highest and fairest. . . .[18]

> Unfortunately, this was all romance—there was no such man. There was indeed, a person of very common, self-interested aims and worldly nature, whom she had credited at sight with an unlimited draft on all her better nature. . . .[19]

Such observations led, for Mrs. Stowe, to no cynical conclusions. She observed the fact and recorded it without idealizing. Her judging the fact, her clinging to the myth, belong only under a discussion of

---

18. H. B. Stowe, *The Minister's Wooing*, pp. 128-129.
19. H. B. Stowe, *The Minister's Wooing*, p. 119.

---

romanticism in her works.

She strikes a somewhat more sombre tone in *Oldtown Folks* when she has her narrator, Holyoke, say:

> One must be very much of a woman for whom a man can sacrifice the deepest purpose of his life without awaking to regret it. I do not say that my father did so and yet I could see, from the earliest of my recollection, that ours was a household clouded by suppressed regrets, as well as embarrassed by real wants.[20]

Such observations lend themselves to no light touch in *The Pearl of Orr's Island* either, in which she treats the characters and emotions of Moses and Mara with befitting seriousness:

> There are persons often brought into near contact by the relations of life, and bound to each other by a love so close, that they are indispensable to each other, who yet act upon each other as a file upon a diamond, by a slow and gradual friction, the pain of which is so equable, so constantly diffused through life, as scarcely ever to force itself upon the mind as a reality.[21]

Mrs. Stowe was well aware of the operation of the mother-image and its influence on the male in courtship. John Seymour of *Pink and White Tyranny* is one of the more ignorant fools concerning women to appear in American fiction, as the author well knew; indeed, that circumstance is a basic requirement for her story. He writes to his sister about his fiancée:

---

20. H. B. Stowe, *Oldtown Folks*, p. 12.
21. H. B. Stowe, *The Pearl of Orr's Island*, p. 276.

Lillie remarkably resembles the ivory miniature of
our dear sainted mother. She was very much affected
when I told her of it. I think naturally Lillie has very
much such a character as our mother; though
circumstances, in her case, have been unfavorable to
the development of it.[22]

Fairly transparent, isn't it? We are never shown
what John's mother was like, but we do know that in
marrying the real Lillie, he makes a poor choice and,
the damage being done, lives with it. Mrs. Stowe
writes:

John is in love, not with the actual Lillie Ellis, but
with that ideal personage who looks like his mother's
picture, and is the embodiment of all his mother's
virtues. . . . Men and women both pass through this
divine initiation . . . and find, when they have come
into the innermost shrine, where the divinity ought to
be, that there is no god or goddess there; nothing but
the cold black ashes of commonplace vulgarity and
selfishness. Both of them, when the grand discovery
has been made, do well to fold their robes decently
about them and make the best of the matter. If they
cannot love, they can at least be friendly. They can
tolerate, as philosophers; pity, as Christians; and
finding just where and how the burden of an ill-
assorted union galls the least, can then and there
strap it on their backs, and walk on, not only without
complaint, but sometimes in cheerful and hilarious
spirit.[23]

Fifty years later, with *Man and Superman,* and
eighty years later with *The Adventures of the Black Girl
in Her Search for God,* Bernard Shaw wrote passages of
quite similar tone.

Mrs. Stowe's most thorough biographer, Forrest

22. H. B. Stowe, *Pink and White Tyranny.* p. 278.
23. H. B. Stowe, *Pink and White Tyranny,* p. 298.

Wilson, has written of her:

> But behind the affectionate terms which she could
> address even to strangers, one feels her blue eyes
> weighing and appraising. Her bitterest critics were to
> attack her knowledge of character, especially Southern
> character. They could not have assailed her at a
> stronger point. Character was what she did know, for
> she spent her life reading character.[24]

A perusal of her books tends to corroborate
Wilson's judgment. In her second novel she came close
to describing sublimation:

> Clayton had just passed through one of the great
> crises of life. All there is in that strange mystery of
> what man can feel for woman had risen like a wave
> within him; and gathering into itself for a time the
> whole force of his being, had broken, with one dash,
> on the shore of death, and the waters had flowed
> helplessly backward. In the great void which follows
> such a crisis, the soul sets up a craving and cry for
> something to come in to fill the emptiness; and while
> the heart says no *person* can come into that desolate
> and sacred enclosure, it sometimes embraces a
> *purpose*, as some sort of substitute.[25]

She was perceptive enough not to be fooled by
the person whose virtue consisted merely in obeying
the Thou-shalt-nots. Clayton, the likable and
intelligent hero of *Dred*, speaks the following, but as
usual the reader is certain that the sympathetic
character in the novel speaks for her:

> "A great deal . . . is called goodness which is
> nothing but want of force. A person is said to have

---

24. Forrest Wilson, *Crusader in Crinoline*, New York, J. P. Lippincott Co.,
1941, p. 83.
25. H. B. Stowe, *Dred*, v. ii, p. 147.

---

self-government simply because he has nothing to
govern. They talk about self-denial when their desires
are so weak that one course is about as easy to them
as another. Such people . . . make, as you say, very
stupid, good people.[26]

With a few strokes in *Uncle Tom's Cabin*, Mrs.
Stowe paints a portrait of a neurasthenic in Marie St.
Clare, and moreover, convinces one that she
understands what makes the woman operate. Marie,
she tells us, has never had "much capability of
affection," and what she had has been "merged into
most . . . unconscious selfishness," obtuse and utterly
ignorant of any but its own.

> There is not on earth a more merciless exacter of
> love from others than a thoroughly selfish woman; and
> the more unlovely she grows, the more jealously . . .
> she exacts love. When St. Clare began to drop off those
> gallantries . . . which flowed at first through the
> habitude of courtship . . . there were abundance of
> tears, poutings, small tempests. . . .[27]

The woman is petulantly jealous of St. Clare's
devotion to his new daughter, Eva:

> . . . all that was given to Eva seemed so much
> taken from herself. A life of constant inaction, bodily
> and mental, the friction of ceaseless ennui and
> discontent in the course of a few years changed the
> blooming young belle into a yellow, faded, sickly
> woman, whose time was divided among a variety of
> fanciful diseases, and who considered herself the most
> ill-used and suffering person in existence.[28]

Later, following Eva's and St. Clare's deaths,

26. H. B. Stowe, *Dred*, v. ii, p. 26.
27. H. B. Stowe, *Uncle Tom's Cabin*, v. i, pp. 233-234.
28. H. B. Stowe, *Uncle Tom's Cabin*, v. i, pp. 235.

Miss Ophelia, Augustine's New England aunt, tries to push Marie into freeing Tom, as St. Clare had wished. Marie, true to her character as drawn, takes the petulant, defensive stance:

> "Everybody goes against me! . . . Everybody is so inconsiderate! But nobody ever does consider—my trials are so peculiar! It's so hard, that when I had only one daughter, she should have been taken!—and when I had a husband that just exactly suited me—and I'm so hard to be suited—he should be taken! And you seem to have so little feeling for me, and keep bringing it up to me so carelessly—when you know how it overcomes me!" And Marie sobbed, and gasped for breath, and called Mammy to open the window, and to bring her the camphor bottle, and to bathe her head, and unhook her dress.[29]

Mrs. Stowe gave evidence, too, that she understood sibling jealousy. Nina, heroine of *Dred*, tries to explain to Clayton the rather disagreeable treatment she receives at the hands of her brother:

> . . . my brother never did treat me as if he loved me. I can't tell what the reason is: whether he was jealous of my poor father's love for me . . . or whatever the reason might be—he never has been kind to me long at a time.[30]

At times she shows that half-hidden, or even entirely hidden purposes of the individual irresistibly outflanking the censor; for example:

> . . . from time to time passed long letters between the two friends. Each was firm in the faith that buried love must have no earthly resurrection. Every letter strenuously insisted that they should call each other

---

29. H. B. Stowe, *Uncle Tom's Cabin*, v. ii, pp. 193-194.
30. H. B. Stowe, *Dred*, v. i, p. 177.

---

brother and sister, and under cover of those names the letters grew longer and more frequent. . . .[31]

On another occasion, she has Jonathan Rossiter disarmingly admit at least one of the truths about his motivations:

> I am dictatorial by nature, and one of those who need constantly to see themselves reflected in other people's eyes; and so I have got an academy here, up in the mountains, where I have a set of as clear, bright-eyed, bright-minded boys and girls as you would wish to see, and am in my ways a pope. Well, I enjoy being a pope. It is one of my weaknesses.[32]

Or again she shows that the virtue displayed is in no way the virtue it pretends to be. Grace, in *Pink and White Tyranny*, has quietly assumed the corona of self-abnegation in not marrying, ostensibly because her bachelor brother and widowed father need her. It has been, of course, not unselfishness, but fear and a kind of self-indulgence. Mrs. Stowe feels at least enough of this to put just a hint of it into the rather stupid John Seymour's mind:

> "It is your self-abnegation, you dear over-good woman, that makes us men seem selfish. We should be as good as you are, if you would give us the chance. I think, Gracie, though you're not aware of it, there is a spice of pharisaism in the way you good girls allow us men to swallow you up without ever telling us what you are doing. . . .[33]

Two of her novels, if not more, contain passages clearly indicating her awareness of an unconscious

31. H. B. Stowe, *The Pearl of Orr's Island*, p. 399.
32. H. B. Stowe, *Oldtown Folks*, p. 221.
33. H. B. Stowe, *Pink and White Tyranny*, p. 438.

mind that helps to shape her characters' emotions and to influence their acts.

> The external life is positive, visible, definable, easily made the subject of conversation. The inner life is shy, retiring, most difficult to be expressed in words, often inexplicable, even to the subject of it, yet no less a positive reality than the outward.[34]

Of the ten novels Mrs. Stowe wrote, five concern themselves to a considerable extent with the lives of children. A few examples should serve to indicate that she did not invariably indulge in the sentimentalism that went into little Eva, but was at times able, even in writing about an age which most adults tend to see through a glass rosily, to represent without idealization.

Scarcely a doubt exists that Mrs. Stowe was always acutely aware of having been the sixth in a family of eleven surviving children. Writing *Poganuc People*, at sixty-five, she produced a story in many ways compensatory to herself for a life she had not led. She is, however, in that book, quite clear and probably reminiscent about Dolly Cushing's place in the household. Her depiction of Dolly is credible and often impressive for its insight, stating, for instance, that "at times she sighed over the dreadful insignificance of being only a little girl in a great family of grown-up people," that her brothers, though good-natured, were "prompt to suggest that it was 'time for Dolly to go to bed.'" Grown-ups, she recalls, got civil answers when they asked questions. The child, Dolly, revels in an illness because of which she becomes the center of

---

34. H. B. Stowe, *We and Our Neighbors*, p. 439.

---

attention and has affection lavished upon her:

> The doctor was sent for. Her mother put away all
> her work and held her in her arms. Her father came
> down out of his study and sat up rocking her nearly
> all night, and her noisy, roistering brothers came
> softly to her door and inquired how she was, and Dolly
> was only sorry that the cold passed off so soon, and
> she found herself healthy and insignificant as ever.
> Being gifted with an active fancy, she sometimes
> imagined a scene when she should be sick and die,
> and her father and mother and everybody would cry
> over her, and there would be a funeral for her. . . .[35]

Harry Henderson, narrator and hero of *My Wife
and I*, is the tenth child in a minister's family, born
when "nobody wants or expects" him. Speaking
through him, Mrs. Stowe shows that she is no fool
about the importance and significance of the so-called
little things to a child.

> There were for me . . . bitter disappointments. If
> any company came and the family board was filled
> and the cake and preserves brought out, and gay
> conversation made my heart bound with special
> longings to be in at the fun, I heard them say, "No
> need to set a plate for Harry—he can just as well wait
> till after." I can recollect many a serious deprivation of
> mature life that did not bring such bitterness of soul
> as that sentence of exclusion.[36]

The child Harry is, of course, driven out of his
hiding place in the livingroom when the older girls'
suitors call ("Mamma, mustn't Harry go to bed?") and
his sister's wish, as Mrs. Stowe puts it, "to have the
deck cleared for action, and superfluous members

---

35. H. B. Stowe, *Poganuc People*, pp. 9-10.
36. H. B. Stowe, *My Wife and I*, pp. 8-9.

Harriet Beecher Stowe:

finally disposed of." "Take it all in all," she has Harry say, explaining without much intensity the plight of the tacitly rejected child, "I felt myself, though not wanting in the supply of any physical necessity, to be somehow . . . a very lonesome little fellow."[37]

Discussions and passages of dialogue about the emotions of children and the raising of them occur repeatedly in *Oldtown Folks*, a book which is a better vein of intellectual and sociological lore in Mrs. Stowe's works than it is a novel. Her good angel of child rearing, who is capable of understanding how a child feels, is Grandmother Badger; she is by no means above anger or the retaliatory cuff, followed rather than preceded by the word of precaution, but she has imagination, and gives the child, any child within reach, love along with food, clothing, and shelter. She says:

> "Lucinda Morse ain't a bit better than you are, Lois, if she was whipped and made to lie still when she as a baby, and you were taken up and rocked when you cried. All is, they had hard times when they was little, and cried themselves to sleep nights . . . when they ought to have been taking some comfort. Ain't the world hard enough, without fighting babies, I want to know."[38]

Grandmother Badger skirmishes with the bad angels of cold system and cold judicial punishment: Aunt Lois, who argues for it, and Miss Asphyxia, incapable of comprehending any alternative, who practices it. Of Miss Asphyxia's inexorable use of the rod, Mrs. Stowe writes:

---

37. H. B. Stowe, *My Wife and I*, p. 9.
38. H. B. Stowe, *Oldtown Folks*, p. 245.

Woman and Artist

It is not to be supposed that Miss Asphyxia regarded herself otherwise than as thoroughly performing a most necessary duty. She was as ignorant of the blind agony of mingled shame, wrath, sense of degradation, and burning for revenge which had been excited by her measures, as the icy wind of Boston flats is of the stinging . . . it causes in its course.

There is a class of coldly conscientious, severe persons, who still, as a matter of duty and conscience, justify measures like these in education. *They*, at all events, are the ones who ought to be forbidden to use them, and whose use of them with children too often proves a soul-murder—a dispensation of wrath and death.[39]

Even the coldness and lack of sympathy without punishment have a sufficiently terrifying effect on the seven-year-old Tina in Miss Asphyxia's "desolately orderly and neat home."

"Sit there," she said, "till I'm ready to see to ye."

An irrepressible feeling of desolation came over the child. The elation produced by the ride died away; and as she sat dangling her heels from the chair, and watching the dry, grim form of Miss Asphyxia, a sort of terror of her began slowly to usurp the place of that courage which had at first inspired the child to rise up against the assertion of so uncongenial a power.[40]

Assuredly there are commentators who would place such observations and biases of Mrs. Stowe's under the heading of the sentimental influence, rather than as they are here, under a sense of realism. If such critics are right, then leaders today in pediatrics and psychiatry, and not the lunatic fringes of those

39. H. B. Stowe, *Oldtown Folks*, p. 132.
40. H. B. Stowe, *Oldtown Folks*, p. 102.

schools either, must be held to have fallen under the influence of a sentimental tradition.

Harriet Beecher Stowe was a fluent and uneven writer. The words read as if they had been poured out with little revision and less cutting. Scattered through her pages are a considerable number of phrases, sentences, paragraphs that bear witness to her sense of realism at work on human character and institutions; each seems to be the quick, perceptive flash of an artist rather than the thought-out deduction of a philosopher, and each shows the writer at work on representation without idealization. If another element is added at all, it is wit:

"He was one of that class of people who, of a freezing day, will plant themselves directly between you and the fire, and there stand and argue to prove that selfishness is the root of all moral evil."[41]

The daughter, sister, wife, and mother of ministers, she did not hesitate to turn a barb on church or clergy when she felt it was deserved:

> . . . everything about the services of this church was thoroughly toned down by good breeding. The responses of the worshippers were given in decorous whispers that scarcely disturbed the solemn stillness; for when a congregation of the best-fed and best-bred people of New York on their knees declare themselves "miserable sinners," it is a matter of delicacy to make as little disturbance as possible.[42]

Following a description of the sermon, she

---

41. H. B. Stowe, *The Minister's Wooing*, p. 58.
42. H. B. Stowe, *We and Our Neighbors*, p. 115.

---

writes:

> The greater part of the audience in the intervals of somnolency congratulated themselves that they were in no danger of running after new ideas, and thanked God that they never speculated about philosophy.[43]

There was no compulsion upon her, however, to satirize, and when the situation called merely for unvarnished insight into character, or at most, quiet amusement, she offered just that: "There are some people so evidently broadly and heartily of this world that their coming into a room always materializes the conversation."[44] "Mrs. Brown . . . like all other human beings, resented the implication of not having as many trials in life as her neighbors."[45]

A critic of Mrs. Stowe's work once remarked that she was the only sentimental novelist of her time who had some sense of reality. It may well be that the reverse is also partly true, that she was to a very large extent a purveyor of realism, of representation without idealization, who too often succumbed either to the public demand for the sentimental tone, or to her own taste for it. Her sense of realism, when she allowed it to work, provided the salt of her art and raised it above the level of much of the writing of her time.

43. H. B. Stowe, *We and Our Neighbors*, p. 118.
44. H. B. Stowe, *The Minister's Wooing*, p. 49.
45. H. B. Stowe, *The Minister's Wooing*, pp. 53-54.

IV. FORCE AND COUNTER-FORCE

The theology of Puritanism was of course deduced from the Bible. To the Puritan the word of God was the last word, as well as the first, but there was nothing to prevent one's introducing collateral arguments and reasoning from experience; it was, in fact, one's duty to search for knowledge and exercise reason. Jonathan Edwards, whose *Freedom of the Will*, an attack on the Arminians, was entirely a work of deduction, argument from given premises, turned to the methods of empiricism for *Original Sin*, and attacked his opponents again, this time inductively, observing experience to verify universal law.[1] Discussing the Puritans' view of the world, Perry Miller writes:

> It is obvious that man dwells in a splendid universe, a magnificent expanse of earth and sky and heavens, which manifestly is built upon a majestic plan . . . though man himself cannot grasp it . . . the world does give men food and drink, but it gives grudgingly and when "the world says peace, peace, then suddenly destruction comes upon them as a whirlwind." It is only too clear that man is not good enough to deserve a better; he is out of touch with the grand harmony, he is an incongruous being amid the creatures, a blemish and a blot upon the face of nature. . . . All

1. Perry Miller, *Jonathan Edwards*, New York, William Sloane Associates, Inc., 1949, pp. 266-268.

about him he sees men . . . exemplifying the horrors of their detached and forlorn condition. They murder, malign, and betray each other, they are not to be relied upon, they wear themselves out in the chains of lust, their lives have no meaning, their virtues are pretenses and their vices unprofitable.[2]

Mrs. Stowe at times felt few uncertainties about this matter:

These awful questions underlie all religions—they belong as much to Deism as to the strictest orthodoxy—in fact, they are a part of human perception and consciousness, since it cannot be denied that Nature in her teaching is a more tremendous and inexorable Calvinist than the Cambridge Platform or any other platform. . . .[3]

She was, after all, a daughter of Lyman Beecher, that follower of the thought of Jonathan Edwards for whom Unitarianism was "like a fire in the bones," who in 1828 announced to his Boston congregations: "I stood today by the grave of the Mathers. I looked back to the early days of New England. I called the God of our fathers to witness that I would never give up this battle until the faith of the Puritans was vindicated and accepted among their posterity."[4]

When Lyman Beecher read aloud to his second wife Jonathan Edwards' sermon, "Sinners in the Hands of an Angry God," young Harriet lay curled up on the sofa, ostensibly reading her own book, but actually listening to her father and watching her step-mother's rather violent response. One of her favorite books in her father's study was Mather's *Magnalia*, and another was the great artist-Puritan's allegory,

---

2. Perry Miller, *The New England Mind,* Harvard University Press, 1954, pp. 7-8.
3. H. B. Stowe, *Oldtown Folks,* p. 26.
4. Forest Wilson, p. 76.

Pilgrim's Progress.[5]

Looking back, largely to her own childhood, in *Poganuc People*, Mrs. Stowe has the autobiographical child, Dolly, open the great chimney door in the garret of her New England home:

> Its door . . . glistened with condensed creosote, a rumbling sound was heard there, and loud crackling reverberated within. Sometimes Dolly would open the door . . . and think with a shudder of a certain passage in John Bunyon, which reads:
>
> > "Then I saw in my dreams that the shepherds had them to another place, in a bottom, where was a door in the side of a hill; and they opened the door and bid them look in. They looked in, therefore, and saw that within it was dark and smoky; they also thought that they heard a rumbling noise as of fire and a cry of some tormented, and they smelt the scent of brimstone. Then said Christian, What means this? The shepherds told them, This is a byway to Hell, a way that hypocrites go in at, namely such as sell their birthright with Esau; such as sell their Master with Judas; such as lie and dissemble with Ananias and Sapphira his wife."[6]

Dolly shivers, not perhaps without a certain perverse pleasure, but is much relieved all the same, when Nappy Higgins hauls her away and extracts from the chimney "a very terrestrial and substantial ham."

The pre-adolescent girl who had peered into the chimney, who had watched her father conduct numerous revivals, who wrote, as a school essay, "Can the Immortality of the Soul be Proved by the Light of Nature?" was by no means ignorant of her position in a Calvinist universe:

---

5. Charles Edward Stowe and Lyman Beecher Stowe, Harriet Beecher Stowe, Boston, Houghton Mifflin Co., 1911, pp. 12-13.
6. H. B. Stowe, *Poganuc People*, pp. 118-119.

She had not sat through the long hours of Meeting every Sabbath morning, and recited the Assembly Catechism every Sabbath afternoon for ten years . . . without learning that she was a child of sin shapen in iniquity; without learning, also, what was expected of her if she would escape eternal punishment. She must first have a conviction of sin, a sense of herself as a depraved being, utterly devoid of holiness, and then complete faith in the power of God to redeem her if He would.[7]

But Lyman Beecher was a Calvinist who believed the prime purpose of his call was not theology, not preaching, but saving souls, whose favorite message was one of God's love, who was capable of "forgetting his doctrinal subtleties," and speaking "with all the simplicity and tenderness of a rich nature concerning the faithful, generous, tender love of Christ."[8]

Thanks at least in part to having such a father, Harriet Beecher experienced conversion in 1825, when she was fourteen. Lyman Beecher wrote in a letter that Mary and Harriet "now stand propounded," and later, "Mary and Harriet communed today for the first time, and it has been a powerful and delightful day."[9]

Two years later, upon joining a Hartford church, Harriet entered upon a period of self-examination and self-accusation of sin, a period of doubts and morbid speculations. The minister examining her evidences said:

"Harriet, do you feel that if the universe should be destroyed (awful pause) you could be happy with God alone?" . . . the child of fourteen stammered out, "Yes

---

7. Catherine Gilbertson, p. 26.
8. Catherine Gilbertson, p. 36, who is paraphrasing *Poganuc People*, p. 208.
9. Catherine Gilbertson, p. 36.

sir."

"You realize, I trust," continued the doctor, "in some measure at last, the deceitfulness of your heart, and that in punishment for your sins God might justly leave you to make yourself as miserable as you have made yourself sinful?"

"Yes sir," again stammered Harriet.[10]

Later, out of her misery and mental torment, she wrote to her brother Edward:

My whole life is one continued struggle: I do nothing right. I yield to temptation almost as soon as it assails me. My deepest feelings are very evanescent. I am beset behind and before, and my sins take away all my happiness. But that which most constantly besets me is pride—I can trace almost all my sins back to it.

From this slough of despond she did not altogether emerge until her twenties.[11] Indeed, there is some question that she emerged so soon, for Charles Foster states that in May 1832, as a matter of spiritual retreat, she wrote her friend Georgiana of her plan to live externally, and that while at Cincinnati she went through further mental struggles in sympathy with her brother Charles, who had grounded on the ledges of a hopeless fatalism after studying Edwards' Freedom of the Will.[12] At the time of her brother George's death from a shotgun accident in 1843 she was still, or else again, unwilling to submit to God's will, apparently at least for some months. Then: "All changed. . . . The will of Christ seems to me the steady pulse of my being. . . . Skeptical doubt cannot exist. I find I can do all things through Christ."[13] When her baby, Charley,

10. *Life and Letters of Harriet Beecher Stowe*, ed. Annie Fields, Boston, Houghton Mifflin & Co., 1898, pp. 52-53.
11. Forest Wilson, p. 72.
12. C. H. Foster, p. 23.
13. C. H. Foster, p. 24.

Woman and Artist

was mortally ill during an epidemic of Asiatic cholera in 1848, she was able to write her husband, who was in the East: "Bear up. Let us not faint when we are rebuked of Him."[14]

Little wonder it is that a woman with such a spiritual development behind her should, under the pressure of other forces as well, try to reconcile a God of live with an intense sense of sin and spiritual torture from a severe omnipotent Power. Of Legree she writes:

> There is a dread, unhallowed necromancy of evil, that turns things sweetest and holiest to phantoms of horror and affright. That p[ale, loving mother . . . wrought in that demoniac heart of sin only as a damning sentence, bringing with it a fearful looking for of judgment and fiery indignation. Legree burned the hair, and burned the letter; and when he saw them hissing and crackling in the flame, only shuddered as he thought of everlasting fires. He tried to drink and revel, and swear away the memory; but often, in the deep of night, whose solemn stillness arraigns the bad soul in forced communion with herself, he had sen that pale mother rising by his bedside, and felt the soft twining of that hair around his fingers, till the cold sweat would roll down his face, and he would spring from his bed in horror.[15]

The final paragraphs of *Uncle Tom's Cabin* show a more direct response to her Calvinist background. They show no conflict within the author, only a clear-sighted, firm, Puritan statement and constitute a fitting close to a long sermon on the duties of Christians:

---

14. C. H. Foster, p. 26.
15. H. B. Stowe, *Uncle Tom's Cabin*, v. ii, p. 267.

Harriet Beecher Stowe:

But who may abide the day of his appearing? "For that day shall burn as an oven: and he shall appear as a swift witness against those that oppress the hireling in his wages, the widow and the fatherless, and that *turn aside the stranger in his right* and he shall break in pieces the oppressor."

Are not these dread words for a nation bearing in her bosom so mighty an injustice? Christians: every time you pray that the kingdom of Christ may come, can you forget that prophecy associates in dread fellowship the day of vengeance with the year of his redeemed? A day of grace is yet held out to us. Both North and South have been guilty before God; and the Christian Church has a very heavy account to answer. Not by combining together, to protect injustice and cruelty, and making a common capital of sin, is this Union to be saved—but by repentance, justice, and mercy; for, not surer is the eternal law by which the mill-stone sinks in the ocean, than that stronger law by which injustice and cruelty shall bring on nations the wrath of Almighty God![16]

Agnes of Sorrento, Mrs. Stowe's novel about Savonarola's Italy, includes among its characters one Father Francesco, who, to his shock and utter dismay discovers himself falling in love with the young Agnes, and mounts the side of Vesuvious to probe and if possible to cleanse his soul. But it is a Calvinist whom we find approaching the edge of the crater of eternal damnation rather than an Italian cleric. A kind of Hawthornesque evil, ubiquitous and imminent, bubbles up around and at him:

Now and then his foot would crush in, where the lava had hardened in a thinner crust, and he would draw it suddenly back from the lurid, red-hot metal beneath. The staff on which he rested was constantly kindling into a light blaze as it slipped into some heated hollow,

16. H. B. Stowe, *Uncle Tom's Cabin*, v. ii, pp. 381-382.

Woman and Artist

and he was fain to beat out the fire upon the cooler surface.[17]

The analogy is clear enough, dramatizing of course Father Francesco's predicament: he, like a conscientious Puritan, is ever beating out the fires of evil on the surface, but is painfully aware of the lurid glow of evil within his depths. He soliloquizes and suffers torment like a New England Calvinist too, as if purgatory, and divine mercy, and forgiveness were no part of his theology:

> "Ah, God. . . . For this vain life of man! . . . Fools that we are to clamor for indulgence and happiness in this life, when the question is, to escape everlasting burnings! If I tremble at this outer court of God's wrath and justice, what must be the fires of hell? These are but earthly fires; they can but burn the body: those are made to burn the soul; they are undying as the soul is. What would it be to be dragged down, down into an abyss of soul-fire hotter than this for ages on ages? This might bring merciful death in time; that will have no end."[18]

As will be seen in comments on the other novels, Mrs. Stowe had observed, and for a long time, apparently, thought about those people whose robust, matter-of-fact, and essentially optimistic natures persist in seeing only the obviously good in God, the love in everything, who persist in a kind of magnificent and beautiful ignoring of preaching, and, half the time at least, she would add, of experience. A peasant, concerned for Father Francesco's well-being, follows the monk up Vesuvius to bring him food. For this peasant, the fires of Vesuvius suggest nothing about

17. H. B. Stowe, *Agnes of Sorrento*, p. 257.
18. H. B. Stowe, *Agnes of Sorrento*, p. 258.

the horrors of eternal damnation; they present, rather, an opportunity to bake an egg! "Our good God gives us our fire for nothing here." Mrs. Stowe never ceases to be amazed and delighted over this type of human being, whose spiritual journey seemed to comfortable.

> Could there be, in the spirit of such persons, a solution to the philosopher's problem of evil? Was it they who held the key for reconciling a revengeful and loving a loving Father? There was something wholesomely kindly and cheerful in the action and expression of the man, which broke upon the overstrained and disturbed musings of the monk like daylight on a ghastly dream. The honest, loving heart sees love in everything; even the fire is its fatherly helper, and not its avenging enemy.[19]

Deacon Twitchell in *The Minister's Wooing* stands at the other extreme, painfully introspective in his search for disinterested benevolence. A shiftless neighbor sends word on a winter night that she is sick and needs firewood. The Deacon gets up, dresses, and prepares for the trip.

> "Says I, 'Father, you know you'll be down with the rheumatic for this; besides, Beulah is real aggravatin'. I know she trades off what we send her to the store for rum, and you never get no thanks. She expects, 'cause we has done for her, we always must; and more we do, more we may do.' And says he to me, says he, 'That's jest the way we sarves the Lord, Polly; and what if He shouldn't hear us when we call on Him in our troubles?' So I shet up; and the next day he was down with the rheumatis. And Corinthy Ann, says she, 'Well, father, *now* I hope you'll own you've got *some* disinterested benevolence,' says she; and the Deacon he thought it over a spell, and then he says, 'I'm afraid it's all selfish. I'm jest a-askin' a righteousness of

---

19. H. B. Stowe, *Agnes of Sorrento*, p. 260.

---

it.' "20

Frequently Mrs. Stowe mixed these probings and examinations in the dish of New England humor, but she was none the less serious for that. In *Oldtown Folks* she turned her attention again to the effect of Puritan theology on the individual soul, a phenomenon she had witnessed, had herself felt, and for long was unable to release.

> On some natures theology operates as a subtle poison; and the New England theology in particular, with its intense clearness, its sharp-cut crystalline edges and needles of thought, has had in a peculiar degree the power of lacerating the nerves of the soul and producing strange states of morbid horror and repulsion.[21]

In particular was she concerned over the high hurdle which the great Jonathan Edwards had placed before each Christian?

> Jonathan Edwards, a man who united in himself the natures of both a poet and a metaphysician . . . fell into the error of making his own constitutional religious experience the measure and standard of all others. . . .
> Regeneration, as he taught it . . . was the implantation by Divine power of a new spiritual sense in the soul, as diverse from all the other senses as seeing is from hearing, or tasting from smelling. No one that had not received this supernatural sense could properly belong to the Church of Christ, and all men, until they did receive it, were naturally and constitutionally enemies of God.[22]

---

20. H. B. Stowe, *The Minister's Wooing*, pp. 47-48.
21. H. B. Stowe, *Oldtown Folks*, p. 26.
22. H. B. Stowe, *Oldtown Folks*, p. 365.

There comes a time in the writing of Mrs. Stowe when the force of Puritanism seems to have been spent, or at least to have dropped into the background where it deals no more pain, as will be discussed later, but even in what may be called her New York novels, its nearly indestructible force crops up.

Ida Van Arsdel, a New Yorker of a New England family, has still some of the old way of life in her. She is the daughter who eschews society, who prefers merely old, not antique furniture, and prepares herself for a profession.

> "I like hardness and simplicity. I am sick to death of softness and perfumed cushions and ease. . . . I want to live while I live, and to keep myself in such trim that I can *do* something—and I won't pet myself or be petted."
> "There," said Eva, laughing, "blood will tell; there's the old Puritan broken loose in Ida. She don't believe any of their doctrines but she goes on their track. . . . Ida is as bent on testifying and going against the world as any old Covenanter."[23]

So also Harry Henderson's cousin Caroline, of both *My Wife and I* and *We and Our Neighbors* finds she must have a skill, partly for self-support, "and more than that, as a refuge from morbid distresses of mind which made the still monotony of my New England country life intolerable to me. . . ."[24]

One glance at her biography will show any reader that there is nothing astonishing about the strength and force of Puritanism as it stormed through the novels of Harriet Beecher Stowe. It could have done little else. Its timbre and its entwined path

---

23. H. B. Stowe, *My Wife and I,* p. 194
24. H. B. Stowe, *My Wife and I,* p. 79.

---

through both her life and her art have been excellently traced by Charles H. Foster in *The Rungless Ladder.*

But there was still another power, a very general and nearly universal one, that threw its weight too into the balance. Without it, the tension that created the best as well as most interesting of her novels might never have existed. In an essay, "Montana: or the End of Jean-Jacques Rousseau," Leslie Fiedler states that behind the thin, neoclassical facade of the eastern seaboard "the mythical meanings of America have traditionally been sustained by the Romantic sensibility; . . ."[25] America, he says, has been "unremittingly dreamed from East to West as a testament to the original goodness of man. . . ." And Foster, touching upon the effect of romanticism on American letters, speaks of "the heady excitement produced by the conjunction of democracy and the romanticism coming to New England via Coleridge and Carlyle," and the "romantic and platonic idealism in the air."[26] Near to the closing page of *The Rungless Ladder* he writes:

> Obviously the major writers of our American Renaissance were powerfully influenced by English, French, and German romanticism, either directly or indirectly, and profoundly shaped by democratic doctrine. But when we read the novels of Harriet Beecher Stowe, particularly her New England novels, we discover again and again in her people habits of thought and feeling and action which remind us of Emerson and Thoreau, Dickinson, Hawthorne, and Melville. Admittedly Harriet, like her more artful contemporaries was expressing an almost universally

25. Leslie Fiedler, *An End to Innocence*, Boston, The Beacon Press, 1955, p. 132.
26. C. H. Foster, p. 190.

Harriet Beecher Stowe:

diffused romanticism.[27]

If romanticism includes the recognition of the reality, Mrs. Stowe's sense of realism often equipped her to take that basic step. Her Puritan upbringing virtually guaranteed her passing judgment upon the reality. The myth, to which it was stipulated in chapter I the romanticist clings, includes a series of ideas or attitudes that together helped make up that "universally diffused romanticism." Among them are an assumption of the original goodness of human beings, the concept of the noble savage, the idea of nature as a moral teacher, of the equal rights of man, of the holy right of the perceptive and noble individual to rebel against society, and of a reliance upon intuition, instinct, or impulse, as guides to living.

Of nineteenth century literature, Fred Lewis Pattee writes:

> The nineteenth century both in Europe and America was a period of revolt, of breakings away from tradition, of voices in the wilderness. It was the age of Byron; and Shelley, of Carlyle and Tolstoy, of Heine and Hugo. Literature came everywhere as the voice of revolution. It rang with protest—Dickens and George Eliot, Kingsley, Whittier, and Mrs. Stowe; it dreamed of a new social era—Fourier and the sons of Rousseau in France, the Transcendentialists in America; it let itself go in romantic abandon and brought back in a flood of feeling and sentiment—thespatromanticker and Bulwer-Lytton and Longfellow. Everywhere conviction, intensity, travail of soul.[28]

As a girl, Harriet Beecher read Byron's

27. C. H. Foster, p. 242.
28. Fred Lewis Pattee, *A History of American Literature Since 1870*, New York, The Century Co., 1915, p. 186.

Woman and Artist

"Manfred," "The Corsair," and "Childe Harold."

> . . . it was the height of the Byron fever in America, and rare was the instructed youth not caught up by it. The new century having swept away the last traces of the old, the young men of Judge Reeve's law school were affecting Byronic collars and cravats. the tender bosoms of Miss Pierce's young ladies were sighing over "Childe Harold" and "Manfred," and not one more deeply than that of Harriet Beecher, on the threshold of adolescence, as she fell in love with an angelic face linked to a heavenly talent, linked also—and more fascinating for it—to sins beyond the ken of a Congregationalist child in Litchfield, Connecticut.[29]

Lyman Beecher, who himself grew enthusiastic over them, urged his children to read Scott's novels,[30] and for Harriet certainly never needed to urge twice. Mrs. Stowe mentions, in *Poganuc People*, these same writers as making up part of the library of the Cushing home and adds to the list Southey and Wordsworth.[31]

She quotes Wordsworth quite frequently, on one occasion employing lines from "Toussaint l'Ouverture,"[32] which, since she asked her publisher to verify them,[33] she must have written from memory. She uses a short quotation from "Tintern Abbey" in the chapter of *The Minister's Wooing* following Mary's betrothal to Dr. Hopkins;[34] and part of "She Was a Phanton of Delight" appears in *Pink and White Tyranny*.[35] Again there is evidence that the author was relying on memory without research, for one line is

29. Forrest Wilson, p. 59.
30. Forrest Wilson, p. 58.
31. H. B. Stowe, *Poganuc People*, pp. 90-91.
32. H. B. Stowe, *Dred*, v. ii, p. 299.
33. Forrest Wilson, p. 418.
34. H. B. Stowe, *The Minister's Wooing*, p. 424.
35. H. B. Stowe, *Pink and White Tyranny*, p. 312.

misquoted and two lines in the middle of a stanza are omitted without indication or comment. Finally, *My Wife and I* has buried within it a quotation from "Ode on Intimations of Immortality," praising, of all things, Central Park.[36] The appearance of these quotations, and there are others, is significant, of course, only insofar as it indicates Mrs. Stowe's familiarity with the works of Wordsworth.

Not so much do the quotations, however, mark her to some extent a romanticist as does her espousal of essentially romantic ideas and attitudes. Her treatment of Clayton, the decent, idealistic Southerner of *Dred* who wishes to ameliorate, and finally eradicate, slavery, at least on his own plantation, is clearly sympathetic throughout. He and the heroine, Nina, attend a camp meeting in North Carolina. When Nina takes exception to its vulgarity and wild freedom, Clayton, linking the superiority of nature over culture in art, religion, and politics, says: ". . . I think there is advantage in everything that stirs up the soul. . . . I listen to music, see pictures, as far as I can, uncritically. . . . So I present myself to all religious exercises. It is the most mysterious part of our nature. I do not pretend to understand it, therefore never criticize."[37]

Nature the moral teacher exerts its influence over one of Cripps children in the same novel, thus;

> Everything was so still, so calm, so pure, no wonder she was prepared to believe that the angels of the Lord were to be found in the wilderness. They who have walked in closest communion with nature have ever

---

36. H. B. Stowe, *My Wife and I,* p. 38.
37. H. B. Stowe, *Dred,* v. i, p. 309.

Woman and Artist

found that they have not departed thence.[38]

Harry Henderson, narrator of *My Wife and I*, usually slips into his story that "The cold mountain air and simple habits of New England country life are largely a preventive of open immorality;"[39] and praises New York's Central Park as "an immortal poem, forever addressing itself to the ear and eye. It is a Wordsworth immortalized and made permanent, preaching to the citizens." "Who shall interpret what is meant by the sweet jargon of robin and oriole and bobolink, with their endless reiterations?" asks the author in *Poganuc People*." Something wiser, perhaps than we dream of in our lower life here."[40]

In one sense, both *Uncle Tom's Cabin* and *Dred* are novels concerning, at least in part, romantic rebels against an evil society. The tradition was already well established: Blake sported a cockade in London streets; Wordsworth had his French tutor of revolutionary ethics, the army officer who talked earnestly to him on those walks along the Loire; Wordsworth, Coleridge, and Southey once laid plans for a utopian community in Pennsylvania; Byron went to Greece to support the cause of freedom and died there.

Lyman Beecher had been a great admirer of Byron as genius, and the young Harriet glamorized him (just as did uncounted numbers of other young women) in many a fantasy. There is a touch of the Byronic in Augustine St. Clare. He has the clear, caustic mind, the satirical touch, wit, good looks, and

---

38. H. B. Stowe, *Dred*, v. ii, p. 167.
39. H. B. Stowe, *My Wife and I*, p. 38.
40. H. B. Stowe, *Poganuc People*, p. 129.

---

wealth. He is a harsh critic of society, and an equally harsh critic of himself as part of that society. He even dies young.

St. Clare's verbal lunges are made not alone at the peculiar institution, but at any segment of society that exploits people, and he executes them with a certain spirited and righteous hate that smacks of the romantic's casting down his gauntlet in the face of the world.

> "I declare to you," said he, suddenly stopping before his cousin . . . "there have been times when I have thought, if the whole country would sink, and hide all this injustice and misery from the light, I would willingly sink with it. When I have been travelling up and down on our boats, or about on my collecting tours, and reflected that every brutal, disgusting, mean, low-lived fellow I met, was allowed by our laws to become absolute despot of as many men, women, and children as he could cheat, steal, or gamble money enough to buy—when I have seen such men in actual ownership of helpless children, of young girls and women, I have been ready to curse my country, to curse the human race!"[41]

Speaking of his own family, as well as of others, St. Clare says: "Now an aristocrat, you know, the world over, has no human sympathies, beyond a certain line in society. . . ."[42]

He explains to his Aunt Ophelia what his brother's case for slavery is:

> ". . . *the right of the strongest; he says* . . . that the American planter is 'only doing, on another form, what the English aristocracy and capitalists are doing by the lower classes'; that is, I take it, appropriating them, body and bone, soul and spirit, to their use and convenience. . . . He says there can be no high

41. H. B. Stowe, *Uncle Tom's Cabin*, v. ii, pp. 34-35.

civilization without enslavement of the masses, wither nominal or real. . . . So he reasons, because, as I said, he is born an aristocrat;—so I don't believe because I was born a democrat."[43]

He explains elsewhere that he is a democrat because of home training, his mother having "burnt into my very soul . . . an idea of the dignity and worth of the meanest human soul."[44]

Clayton, the idealist hero of *Dred*, turns, very nearly alone, against a society that is not good enough. He will not be trader, or doctor, or lawyer, although he is trained for the last, because

"I must either lower my standard of right and honor, and sear my soul in all its nobler sensibilities, or I must be what the world calls an unsuccessful man. There is no path in life, that I know of, where humbuggery and fraud and deceit are not essential to success—none where a man can make the purity of his moral nature the first object. . . ."[45]

At this, his friend, Russell, suggests the ministry, to which Clayton replies:

"I'm afraid I should meet him [the Devil] there too. I could not gain a right to speak in my pulpit without some profession or pledge to speak this or that, that would be a snare to my conscience, preach myself out of pulpits quicker than I should plead out at the bar."

Clayton proceeds with his plans to educate his slaves in preparation for the freedom he will grant them and is physically attacked by a small mob. He tries to attain justice in court for an injured Negro and sees his decision reversed by his own father on the

42. H. B. Stowe, *Uncle Tom's Cabin*, v. ii, p. 37.
43. H. B. Stowe, *Uncle Tom's Cabin*, v. ii, p. 45.
44. H. B. Stowe, *Uncle Tom's Cabin*, v. ii, p. 41.
45. H. B. Stowe, *Dred*, v. i, pp. 26-27.

superior bench. He attempts to push a group of ministers into urging legal reform regarding the position of Negroes in court, and is deserted. He is indefatigable at knocking his head against the social wall, but after a hostile crowd burns down the schoolhouse on his plantation, he removes, slaves and all, to Canada where under his leadership they form a thriving community of free men.[46]

Dred himself is also part of the overflow of the romantic movement, not as a social democrat, or idealist, but as a fanatical saver of the oppressed, who is half noble savage, a reader of the messages of God in the leaves of the trees. A swamp dweller, an escaped slave, and a species of Negro Robin Hood, Dred is at the same time a planner of slave revolt, and a spouter of grim and bloody apocalyptic utterances culled from the Bible.

Mrs. Stowe writes at times in *Agnes of Sorrento* with the familiar tones of the social democrat. Implicit in this historical romance is the idea, not very surprising in any American, and especially not in one that had, since childhood, herd solemn annual readings of the Declaration, that good men have the right, nay, almost the moral duty, to rebel against a corrupt government; and that there is something nearly immoral about a people's permitting its own extreme exploitation.

> Meanwhile the mute, subservient common people looked on all this as a part of their daily amusement. Meek dwellers in those dank, noisome caverns, without any opening but a street-door, which are called dwelling-places in Italy, they lived in

46. H. B. Stowe, *Dred*, v. ii, p. 331.

uninquiring good-nature, contentedly bringing up
children on coarse bread, dirty cabbage-stumps, and
other garbage, while all that they could earn was
sucked upward by capillary attraction to nourish the
extravagance of those upper classes on which they
stared with such blind and ignorant admiration.[47]

Her attitude toward all her characters in *Agnes
of Sorrento* not only exonerates the rebel but, still in
the tradition of the romantic movement, idealizes him
too. Hard-riding, bold, dashing, and handsome
Agostino Sarelli has become a chivalric Italian bandit
because his family's property has been confiscated and
he himself has been excommunicated. Like Harriet
Beecher Stowe, Sarelli is torn between reason and
impulse:

> Agostino was like a man who lives in an eternal
> struggle of self-justification—his reason forever going
> over and over with its plea before his regretful and
> never-satisfied heart, which was drawn every hour of
> the day by some chain of memory towards the faith
> whose visible administrators he detested with the
> whole force of his moral being.[48]

He becomes a believer in the "true church of
Christ," as opposed to the corrupt Vatican, and from
Father Antonio, a follower of the excommunicated
Savonarola, he takes communion. Social and religious
rebellion here becomes not only *au fait*, but holy.

The concept of the original goodness of humans
appears, at first glance, with its unavoidable attention
to total depravity, completely alien to all the

---

47. H. B. Stowe, *Agnes of Sorrento*, p. 302.
48. H. B. Stowe, *Agnes of Sorrento*, pp. 120-121.

Harriet Beecher Stowe:

upbringing of Harriet Beecher Stowe. Yet one must not forget the kind of Calvinism that was Dr. Beecher's; he was a man with a cheerful and vigorous passion for saving souls. Mr. Avery, the minister of Cloudland in *Oldtown Folks*, is obviously modelled upon him, and of Mr. Avery Mrs. Stowe writes:

> Mr. Avery was a firm believer in hell, but he believed also that nobody need go there, and he was determined, so far as he was concerned, that nobody should go there if he could help it.[49]

In a universe where the possibility of escape is as nearly indiscriminate as this, the germ of the idea of original goodness might, despite original sin, find a cranny of fertile scuffings and put forth roots. It must have been in some such way that the concept, aided and abetted by the writing and speaking of the times, crept into the mind of Mrs. Stowe, and, often in a form far from clear, and frequently contradicted in other passages, crept also into her novels.

Tom Loker, slave pursuer of *Uncle Tom's Cabin*, after being wounded by Harris and one Quaker, is nursed back to health by another Quaker. Tom's response to this kindness is to give up slave hunting and become a trapper in one of the new settlements,[50] a move, presumably, at least in the direction of greater humanity, and indicating an ability on his part to move back toward a primeval goodness. Augustine St. Clare reports a somewhat similar experience with a lazy, stealing, and violent slave whom he bought from his brother after the chattel had been shot and

---

49. H. B. Stowe, *Oldtown Folks*, p. 143.
50. H. B. Stowe, *Uncle Tom's Cabin*, v. ii, p. 283.

---

wounded in a slave hunt.

> "I took him in hand, and in one fortnight I had him tamed down as submissive and tractable as heart could desire."
>
> "What in the world did you do to him?" said Marie.
>
> "Well, it was quite a simple process. I took him to my room, had a good bed made for him, dressed his wounds, and tended him myself, until he got on his feet again. . . . I had free papers made out for him and told him he might go where he liked.
>
> "He . . . tore the paper in two and absolutely refused to leave me. I never had a braver, better fellow—trusty and true as steel. He embraced Christianity afterwards and became as gentle as a child."[51]

Tomtit, a sort of male Topsy, in *Dred*, is a great trial to nearly everyone on the plantation because of his mischievous evil, but Lisette feels sure the original goodness in him can be made dominant. "I know I could make him good, if I had the care of him."[52] And of Polly, Cripps' second wife in the same book, a woman clearly scraped from the bottom of the barrel of drunken and tawdry poor-whites, Mrs. Stowe writes:

> Whatever she might have been naturally—whatever of beauty or of good there might have been in the womanly nature within her—lay wholly withered and eclipsed under the force of an eduction churchless, schoolless, with all the vices of civilization without its refinements and all the vices of barbarism without the occasional nobility by which they are sometimes redeemed.[53]

Moses of *The Pearl of Orr's Island* is, we are told, a religious skeptic, but not without "the angel in him."

51. H. B. Stowe, *Uncle Tom's Cabin*, v. ii, p. 52.
52. H. B. Stowe, *Dred*, v. i, p. 79.
53. H. B. Stowe, *Dred*, v. ii, pp. 158-159.

He has, Mrs. Stowe says, "the longing after the good and beautiful, which is God's witness in the soul."[54] There is indication also that Maggie, the prostitute of *We and Our Neighbors*, is looked upon by the author as having been originally good. "Nobody wants to be sold under sin, and go the whole length in iniquity."[55] Mrs. Stowe speaks of the "factitious and unnatural life" Lillie Ellis, of *Pink and White Tyranny*, has led and writes that "the whole course of her education had been directed to suppress what little [capacity for love] she had, and to concentrate all her feelings upon herself."[56]

For the Puritan the word of God was the guide for action. The romanticist turned to intuition, impulse, instinct. The two sources were often thought of as far apart; indeed, instinct was for the Puritan closely linked to total depravity. But the word of God came not only through the Bible, not only from the pulpit, but through prayer and introspection, close neighbors to the intuitive revelation. From intuition it is but a step to impulse, and another to instinct. Some even made the transition to simple emotions, but not Mrs. Stowe, who was revolted by the shallow application of a valuable idea for purposes of self-indulgence. In *Pink and White Tyranny* she takes a paragraph for the purpose of ridiculing a group of city socialites among whom it is understood that "the religion of the emotions is the only true religion."

> Although it was well understood among them that
> . . . nothing is holy that you do not feel exactly like

54. H. B. Stowe, *The Pearl of Orr's Island*, p. 230.
55. H. B. Stowe, *We and Our Neighbors*, pp. 328-329.
56. H. B. Stowe, *Pink and White Tyranny*, p. 519.

doing, and everything is holy that you do; still these fair confessors lacked the pluck of primitive Christians, and could not think of taking joyfully the spoiling of their goods, even for the sake of a kindred spirit. Hence the necessity of living in deplored marriage bonds with husbands who could pay rent and taxers, and stand responsible for unlimited bills at Stewart's and Tiffany's. Hence the philosophy which allowed the possession of the body to one man and of the soul to another, which one may see treated of at large in any writings of the day.[57]

With an occasional exception, Mrs. Stowe's characters do more than yield to mere emotion; the frequency of their reliance upon impulse, upon instinct, is impressive. Of Tiff, the elderly Negro housekeeper in *Dred*, she writes:

After all, Tiff's method of education, instinctive as it was, was highly philosophical, since a certain degree of self-respect is the nurse of many virtues. . . .[58]

Nina, in the same book, refuses to take any part in a legal but questionable manoeuvre because, she says, "I can't prove it's wrong, I shall always feel it is."[59] In *Uncle Tom's Cabin* the writer indicates that the frequent and imaginative visions of the slaves are revelations from God,[60] a conclusion that would have delighted William Blake, and in *We and Our Neighbors*, the reasonable and hard-headed Dr. Campbell, not infrequently acts humanely, against his own reason, and says he does so on instinct:

"I go in for saving in my line by an instinct apart from my reason, an instinct as blind as nature's when she

---

57. H. B. Stowe, *Pink and White Tyranny*, p. 452.
58. H. B. Stowe, *Dred*, v, ii, p. 80.
59. H. B. Stowe, *Dred*, v, i, p. 202.

---

sets out to heal a broken bone in the right arm of a scalawag, who never used his arm for anything but thrashing his wife and children. . . . I have the blind instinct of healing in my profession, and I confess to sitting up all night, watching to keep the breath of life in sick babies that I know had better be dead. . . ."[61]

Lines in *The Minister's Wooing* set forth the ideal of the intuitive truth in religious terms:

Nay, there have been those, undoubtedly, who have known God falsely with the intellect, yet felt Him truly with the heart—and there be many, principally among the unlettered little ones of Christ's flock, who positively know that much that is dogmatically propounded to them . . . is cold, barren, unsatisfying, and utterly false, who yet can give no account of their certainties better than that of the inspired fisherman, "We know Him and have seen Him."[62]

The impulses and religious intuitions of Esther in *Oldtown Folks* are in almost continual combat with her theology and reasoning power, which they ultimately defeat.

Goody Smith, in the same novel, bears false witness, out of instinctive kindness to a child, and suffers neither repentance nor damnation so far as the reader learns.

Sweetcakes were slipped into his hands at all odd intervals, choice morsels set away for his consumption in secret places of the buttery, and many an adroit lie told to Old Crab to secure for him extra indulgences, or prevent the imposition of extra tasks; and many a little lie did she recommend to him, at which the boy's honest nature and Christian education inclined him greatly to wonder.[63]

60. H. B. Stowe, *Uncle Tom's Cabin*, v, ii, p. 296.
61. H. B. Stowe, *We and Our Neighbors*, pp. 266-267.
62. H. B. Stowe, *The Minister's Wooing*, p. 426.
63. H. B. Stowe, *Oldtown Folks*, p. 125.

The author does not exactly exonerate Goody Smith for bearing false witness, but Goody remains a sympathetic character and is not condemned. She understands that Harry needs love, and protection from Crab Smith, and on impulse she breaks all the rules to provide both. Harry is the one whose theology is entirely of the heart, who enthrones there the Second Person of the Trinity, the God of Love, and knows no other. Mrs. Stowe sees in him the fortunate character naturally endowed with grace.[64] Grandmother Badger, who adopts him, expresses an intuitive and impulsive love and humanity often at odds with the strict Calvinist theology she loves to argue. Eva Van Arsdel, of *My Wife and I*, complains not very surprisingly that the line between right and wrong is often difficult to distinguish exactly: "It is the office of common sense . . . to get the exact right in all such matters—there is a sort of *instinct* in it."[65]

Like no small number of other heroines in Mrs. Stowe's novels, Agnes (Of Sorrento) when she does the "right" thing follows the lead of intuition or impulse. She turns to "Him who some divine instinct told her was alone mighty to save."[66]

When George Sand, introducing *Uncle Tom's Cabin* to France in December, 1852, wrote, "Mrs. Stowe is all instinct," she was, intentionally or not, exaggerating.[67] No more, of course, should one call Harriet Beecher Stowe all instinct, or a thoroughly romantic novelist than one should label her thoroughly Puritan. No less than the work of many other writers,

---

64. H. B. Stowe, *Oldtown Folks*, p. 259.
65. H. B. Stowe, *My Wife and I*, p. 281.
66. H. B. Stowe, *Agnes of Sorrento*, p. 346.
67. *Life and Letters of Harriet Beecher Stowe*, p. 154.

Harriet Beecher Stowe:

hers resists being pigeon-holed in any precise category. Among these currents and crosscurrents, between the sense of realism and the cloak of sentimentalism, between Puritanism and romanticism, what were the results in literary art?

V. THE TENSION

According to Mrs. Stowe, she did not write *Uncle Tom's Cabin* . The scenes came before her in a series of visions which she put down in words.[1] Her varying reports of the writing, which contradict one another in material details, consistently lend support to her indication that God guided her hand, or, if one prefers a less religious terminology, that the book was subconsciously planned. This book, and *Dred*, which was published years later, set themselves apart from her other novels, not solely because they are examinations of slavery, but because in them the Puritan and the romantic approach to life concurred, or could be made to concur, in a condemnation of the peculiar institution. Calvinism could be used to support an argument for an hierarchy, no doubt, and for higher and lower forms of human life, but it was difficult to argue from it for the perpetuation of ignorance, for the restriction of Bible reading, or for the sins of adultery, anger, and pride that Mrs. Stowe saw as all too frequently integral parts of the system.

The romantic movement, which had very nearly sprung into existence with its enthroning of the rebel, of individualism, and original goodness of humans,

---

1. *Life and Letters of Harriet Beecher Stowe*, p. 163.

and with its casting society in the role of the corrupting agent, was an even more likely weapon in the arsenal of one bent on ending slavery. Both forces apparently channelled themselves in the subconscious of Mrs. Stowe, who, during twenty years in Cincinnati, had seen mobs throw type from an Abolition press into the river, had witnessed the fearful escape of slaves, and had helped buy a slave child from a Kentucky estate in order to return it to its free mother. Mrs. Stowe's separation from one of her own children by death in 1848 brought all the force of her nature to bear on the theme in fiction of the bereaved mother. In addition, she and others like her were deeply distressed by the passage of the Fugitive Slave Law, and her sister-in-law, Mrs. Edward Beecher, wrote to her: "Hattie, if I could use a pen as you can, I would write something to make this whole nation feel what an accursed thing slavery is."[2]

She used her pen, as soon as the new baby was old enough to give her sufficient leisure, turning out the installments week by week for the "Era,"[3] and telling Jewett, her prospective publisher who was scared of failure because of the story's running to two volumes, that she couldn't help it, the novel was writing itself. She let God and other forces pour it all out, without much application of critical craftsmanship, if any, bringing to the world its three sets of characters held loosely together by the Jesus figure of Tom: the Harrises embroiled in a Cooperesque pursuit-and-escape pattern, the good slave-holding Shellbys and St. Clare, and the bad, ignorant Yankee

2. *Life and Letters of Harriet Beecher Stowe*, p. 130.
3. *Life and Letters of Harriet Beecher Stowe*, p. 133.

slave-holder, Legree.

The sentimentalism that usurps the deaths of Eva and Augustine had free reign; the writer's sense of the real drove home where it could, while Puritanism as exemplified in the book's final paragraphs, and romanticism, as in St. Clare's bitter attacks against exploitation (both passages quoted in chapter IV) were the driving forces.

The deluge that followed should not greatly concern us here: the eight steam presses running day and night in Boston, the 10,000 copies the first week, the 300,000 the first year, the forty editions in England, the endless translations and dramatizations; nor should the aroused enthusiasm and bitterness concern us, the election of Lincoln (which, Seward claimed, without *Uncle Tom* would never have happened), and secession; for it is not sales, not social protest alone, no matter how worthy, not widespread influence that marks successful literary art. At its best a novel sheds a new light on truth, not just on the surface but beneath the surface, often far beneath. At its best it expands the frontiers of the human spirit, making its say subtly, by intimation, by suggestion, by color, and shade, and tone, carving its effects as music does, by indirection, on the psychic depths.

Mrs. Stowe quite rightly conceived of slavery as a social, not a personal evil, one that enmeshed good and bad, both North and South. Accordingly she wrote the novel of social protest, and did so again with *Dred*. In decades since, a few writers like Koestler, Malraux, or Silone have succeeded in making the protest novel a work of considerable literary value, but this aim and this achievement were beyond Mrs. Stowe.

If the purpose of the book was to change the world, it was assuredly a success, but even that fact does not oblige anyone to exalt it above its literary merits. Commenting on the opening chapters of *The Minister's Wooing* which were published in *The Atlantic Monthly* in December 1859, James Russell Lowell wrote: "It has always seemed to us that the anti-slavery element in the two former novels by Mrs. Stowe [*Uncle Tom's Cabin* and *Dred*] stood in the way of a full appreciation of her remarkable genius. . . ."[4] It stood in the way of a full realization of her genius also. Mrs. Stowe felt no need in her slavery books to probe far below the surface. Where she did try to penetrate her characters very much, the sentimental response that was almost part of the air she breathed took over, making Eva, Tom, and Nina incredibly heavenly, and Legree less than convincing in his too thorough viciousness. This observation is not intended to disparage the good character drawing there is in Aunt Ophelia, Loker, and Friends, the slave cook in the St. Clare kitchen, in Tom Gordon, the Skinflints, the Crippses, most of it fairly near the surface. Although St,. Clare makes a sharp and excellent spokesman, he too at times, like Eva and Tom, falls into the unbelievable, especially with his unusually noble sentiments which one simply cannot accept, not from St. Clare.

These are shortcomings which the author overcame in *The Minister's Wooing*, 1859, a book which dealt not with an outward but with an inward problem. The relationship to her art of certain emotional and religious crises in her own life has been

4. *Life and Letters of Harriet Beecher Stowe*, p. 249.

fully traced in Charles Foster's *The Rungless Ladder.*
Suffice it to say here that crucial for Mrs. Stowe's life
and writing was the accidental drowning of her son
Henry in 1857. Henry had written her: "I may not be
what the world calls a Christian, but I will live such a
life as a Christian ought to live, such a life as every
true man ought to live."[5]

Anxiety beyond the harsh and truly terrifying
trauma of such a bereavement assailed Mrs. Stowe
who, only with difficulty ten years before had gone
through a protracted religious crisis and believed
herself reconciled to the ways of God to man. Now,
understandably, the resentment surged up. She wrote
her sister Catherine:

> If ever I was conscious of an attack of the Devil
> trying to separate me from the love of Christ, it was for
> some days after the terrible news came. I was in a
> state of great physical weakness, most agonizing, and
> unable to control my thoughts. Distressing doubts as
> to Henry's spiritual state were rudely thrust upon my
> soul. It was as if a voice had said to me: "You trusted
> in God, did you? You believed that he loved you! You
> had perfect confidence that He would never take your
> child till the work of grace was mature! Now He has
> hurried him into eternity without a moment's warning,
> without preparation, and where is he?"[6]

Where is he? There was the jagged edge of the
torture. Mrs. Stowe felt weak; she tried to "control her
thoughts":

> They [Dartmouth students] were glad to see us there,
> and I was glad that we could be there. Yet right above
> where their boats were gliding in the evening light lay
> the bend in the river, clear, still, beautiful, fringed

5. *Life and Letters of Harriet Beecher Stowe*, p. 240.

with over-hanging pines, from whence our boy went upward to heaven. To heaven—if earnest, manly purpose, if sincere, deliberate strife with besetting sin is accepted of God, as I firmly believe it is. Our dear boy was but a beginner in the right way. Had he lived, we had hoped to see all wrong gradually fall from his soul as the worn-out calyx drops from the perfected flower.[7]

But she could not wholly erase the word *if* from consciousness. In such situations one keeps repeating, "as I firmly believe it is," simply because one cannot. C. H. Foster, writes:

the human personality could reach full development only when through the operation of Grace the will of Christ became the steady pulse of its existence. Henry had not yet passed the critical stage.[8]

Henry Stowe was, "by the logic of his mother's Calvinism, almost certainly in hell."[9]

Catherine Beecher in her youth had lost at sea a fiance who was not a converted Christian, and trying to put her mind at ease, she had searched at length through his letters and journals for some neglected sign of grace. She never found it, and in essays during the years that followed she first edged away from and then, in her refutation of Edwards' philosophy of determinism, rejected the Calvinist doctrine of damnation of such essentially good people who had not experienced Christian conversion.[10] Harriet, faced now with a similar spiritual crisis, laid aside unfinished her few chapters of *The Pearl of Orr's Island* and wrote *The Minister's Wooing*, the romance of an

6. *Life and Letters of Harriet Beecher Stowe*, pp. 243-244.
7. *Life and Letters of Harriet Beecher Stowe*, p. 242.
8. C. H. Foster, p. 92.
9. C. H. Foster, p. 94.
10. Forrest Wilson, p. 58.

almost mystical young woman of Newport in the 1790s.

Mary Scudder, who has ever arrived at her earnest religious beliefs through intuitive processes, whether she was aware of it or not, is entrapped between suitors: James Marvyn, an extroverted young seaman whose courtship has been secret, and whom both Mary's intuition and body tell her she deeply loves; and the Rev. Samuel Hopkins, a figure borrowed from history and altered by Mrs. Stowe, a man so innocent of the world that he falls in love with Mary under cover of religious emotion without even realizing at first what has happened to him. Marvyn, the unconfirmed near-skeptic is reported lost at sea, so that, like Catherine and Harriet, his mother and fiancée are apparently obliged to think of him as eternally damned, and it is here that Calvinist theology, logically deduced from premises, wars with the sprout of religious liberalism, religion intuitively felt, revealed to the individual as right. All the Puritan training of the Beechers, the reasoning, the heritage of Jonathan Edwards struggles mightily with the romantic movement's angel of intuitive knowledge, of truth from impulse, of grace for the good, the kindly, the loving, without the agonies of severe conversion and reconciliation to the will of a grim Father.

On two continents a king had been shaken off; the heady elixer of individualism filled the air; man had broken shackles preparatory to gorging himself on the natural resources of a new world; and now no unfathomably harsh and stern deity could be left enthroned. For the romanticist the only God was the second Person, the God of love, who would place not too many restrictions on free men, and would then forgive. Candace, slave woman in *The Minister's Wooing*, speaks movingly about her belief in a God of Love, one with Jesus, and puts the case of the romantic movement as operating through Mrs. Stowe perhaps as thoroughly as any character in the book. Mrs. Marvyn, thinking her son damned, cries to Mary:

> "Oh, my wedding day! Why did they rejoice? Brides should wear mourning—the bells should toll for every wedding; every new family is built over this awful pit of despair, and only one in a thousand escapes."[11]

Mary stands aghast and for a moment speechless; then, as the full meaning of the words reaches her she cries: "My God, my God! Oh, where art Thou?" Mrs. Marvyn continues:

> "Dr. Hopkins says that this is all best . . . that God chose it because it was for a greater final good—that He not only chose it but took means to make it certain. . . . They say He does this so that He may show to all eternity, by their example, the evil nature of sin and its consequences! . . . It is not right! Yet they say our salvation depends on our loving God . . . loving Him better than our dearest friends. It is impossible! It is contrary to the laws of my nature! I can never love God! . . . No end!—no bottom!—no shore!—no hope! . . .[12]

It is Candace, the Negro servant, who administers the spiritual antidote to this poison:

> "Honey darlin', ya a'n't right,—dar's adrefful mistake somewhar," she said. "Why, do Lord a'n't like what ye tink—He loves ya, honey! Why, jes' feel how I loves ye—poor ole black Candace—an' I ain't better'n

11. H. B. Stowe, *The Minister's Wooing*, p. 314.
12. *Ibid.*, p. 345.

Him as made me! . . .[13]

The battle had raged in other places besides the mind of Mrs. Stowe. Indeed hers was the site of one of the evening skirmishes of the war, but none the less painful and filled with awe for that, and it is the tension of this crucial struggle between opposed world views that gives the book its strength, its dignity, and its success as a novel.

Mrs. Stowe looks into Mary Scudder's heart, looks at the neighbors in late eighteenth century Newport, and asks them the significant questions about the nature of Nature. Repeatedly the author juxtaposes characters of reason and intuition, of logic and impulse. Thus she writes of Mrs. Marvyn and Mary:

> Hers was a nature more reasoning than creative and poetic; and whatever she believed bound her mind in strictest chains to its logical results. She delighted in the regions of mathematical knowledge, and walked them as a native home; but the commerce with abstract certainties fitted her mind more to be stiffened and enchained by glacial reasonings, in regions where spiritual intuitions are necessary as wings to birds.
>
> Mary was by nature of the class who never reason abstractly, whose intellections all begin in the heart, which sends them colored with its warm lifeline to the brain. Her perceptions of the same subjects were as different from Mrs. Marvyn's as his who revels only in color from his who is busy with the dry details of mere outline. The one mind was arranged like a map, and the other like a picture.[14]

---

13. *Ibid.*, p. 347.
14. *Ibid.*, pp. 341-342.

Mrs. Stowe feels a great pity for the spirits that must walk rather than fly. Their predicament is one of her arguments in the struggle tending away from Calvinism.

> There are in this world two kinds of natures—those that have wings and those that have feet—the winged and the walking spirits. The walking are the logicians; the winged are the instinctive and poetic. Natures that must always walk find many a bog, many a thicket, many a tangled brake, which God's happy little winged birds flit over by noiseless flight. Nay, when a man has toiled till his feet weigh too heavily with the mud of earth to enable him to walk another step, these little birds will often cleave the air in a right line towards the bosom of God, and show the way where he could never have found it.[15]

She is aware that a few rare natures, near mystics, can undergo the rigors of Calvinism and emerge the stronger and mightier for it, but the weak with no adequate intuitive balance against an inexorable logic standing on gloomy premises are ground under.

> Thus it happened, that, while strong spirits walked, palm-crowned with victorious hymns, along those sublime paths, feebler and more sensitive ones lay along the track, bleeding away in life-long despair. Fearful to them were the shadows that lay over the cradle and the grave.[16]

Mrs. Stowe's admirable Dr. Hopkins, having at last realized that he desires his landlady's daughter to wife, makes his proposal through the accepted channel, the widowed mother of Mary Scudder, who

---

15. *Ibid.*, p. 295.
16. *Ibid.*, p. 340.

---

relays it to Mary. The girl, admiring and respecting this great spiritual adviser, and thinking James Marvyn dead, accepts, albeit with some highly credible hesitation. Mrs. Stowe manages to keep the reader sympathetic with the Doctor and yet to make the very idea of this engagement repulsive. Madame de Frontignac, the visiting young French woman, asks Mary if it is not a trifle like taking the veil, this marriage with an altar, and the reader is inclined to agree with her that it is.

James Marvyn's return home, as alive as ever, and a convinced Christian besides, does not resolve the complications of the plot, for Mary, a woman of integrity and honor, having given her word, will not renege. There is, behind this, a Calvinist training that the author respects and makes the reader respect:

> Every prayer, hymn, and sermon, from her childhood, had warned her to distrust her inclinations, and regard her feelings as traitors. ... . She had been taught that there was no feeling so strong but that it might be immediately repressed at the call of duty.[17]

The war, however, is not entirely one-sided. Mrs. Stowe's passages argue mightily for idealized love as a vision of heaven, as a fragment of the holy love of God,[18] for intuition and deep psychic demands as opposed to reason, especially of course the secular reason of a burgeoning materialism; but she also champions the way of life of her fathers and writes of it so earnestly and so eloquently that it wins the reader's respect.

---

17. *Ibid.*, p. 511.
18. *Ibid.*, pp. 121-122.

Harriet Beecher Stowe:

> Never was there a community where the roots of
> common life shot down so deeply, and were so
> intensely grappled around things sublime and eternal.
> The founders of it were a body of confessors and
> martyrs, who turned their backs on the whole glory of
> the visible, to found in the wilderness a republic of
> which the God of Heaven and Earth should be the
> sovereign power.
>   Living an intense, earnest, practical life, mostly
> tilling the earth with their own hands, they yet carried
> on the most startling and original religious
> investigations with a simplicity that might have been
> deemed audacious, were it not so reverential. All old
> issues relating to government, religion, ritual, and
> forms of church organizations having for them passed
> away, they went straight to the heart of things, and
> boldly confronted the problem of universal being. [19]

The conventional love triangle is broken by a minor but well-drawn character who tells the Doctor that his fiancée loves another man. Following some hours of prayer and pain, the good Doctor insists upon releasing Mary from her promise. Being, as he is, the *parfit gentil knight*, he can do no less.

Calvinism has come off not so badly as one might expect. It has the moral victory; it has by the sheer force of logic freed two slaves in the community, has stood up to the local vested interests on the slave question and taken the consequences. True, it has really lost the theological war, but that is a fact Mrs. Stowe was unable to let herself say in so many words. To do so would have been to threaten too many of the emotional foundations of her life. Her forces, conscious and unconscious, probably worked together at their best for this book. The cliché romance is imposed on

---

19. *Ibid.*, pp. 332-333.

Woman and Artist

the whole, of course, and sentimentalism lifts its insipid head in the threatened seduction of Mme. de Frontignac by Aaron Burr; but Mrs. Stowe's sense of realism is present as well, as the passages of characterization show. After Mary accepts the Doctor's proposal, for example, a little frightened at what she has done, she looks into her mirror and tries to argue herself around to approve her act.

> The sad, blue eyes that gazed into Mary's had that look of calm initiation, of melancholy comprehension, peculiar to eyes made clairvoyant by "great and critical" sorrow. They seemed to say to her, "Fulfill thy mission; life is made for sacrifice; the flower must fall before fruit can perfect itself." A vague shuddering of mystery gave intensity to her reverie.[20]

The struggle that is within both writer and heroine gives the novel its strength and depth. It is not, as some have said, a total rejection of Calvinism. Mrs. Stowe could not throw off the old training as lightly as that; in fact, she went on apologizing to herself for what she had done through most of her books. C. H. Foster calls *The Minister's Wooing* a Yes *and* No to the Puritan tradition. If so, the No is stronger than the Yes, but the conflict Mrs. Stowe draws here is never resolved with consistency and logic, as it was by Catherine and Henry Ward Beecher.[21] There is further struggle to come, but it is less heated, less titanic; after it follow the mundane, lowland plains, and then a graceful lea on slightly higher ground from which to look back. With this book Mrs. Stowe had come over a jagged spiritual ridge. As

20. *Ibid.*, pp. 410-411.
21. Forrest Wilson, p. 58.

a novelist she had attained her summit.

Agnes of Sorrento, 1862, is Mrs. Stowe's attempt to treat again the theme of *The Minister's Wooing*, this time in an Italian setting, but she did not know Italy as she did New England, and her sense of realism here never had the chance to work with thoroughly known material.

Agnes is ostensibly an Italian peasant of the time of Savonarola, but a shallow tinge of American Puritanism clouds her character. Like Mary Scudder, she is loved by both a man of God and a man of action;. Like Mary, she fears her lover's damnation in eternity. Sentimental formula controls the plot, and outrageous coincident brings Agnes love, riches, faith in the Church Triumphant, and the revelation of noble descent, all nearly in one neat package.

Superficially the tensions and currents that created such voltage and penetration in *The Minister's Wooing* ought to be present in this story, but the reader feels them not. Mrs. Stowe was removed as a writer from the scenes she knew well, had temporarily worn out perhaps the emotional stimulation that had driven her to compose the Newport story, and was incapable of repeating at once that admirable performance.

Shattered by the death of her son Henry in 1857, she had put aside unfinished her manuscript of *The Pearl of Orr's Island*, returning to it after *The Minister's Wooing* was finished, and writing alternately on *The Pearl* and upon *Agnes of Sorrento*. *The Pearl* suffers from the way it grew, starting to be a series of sketches of Maine island characters, then turning into a novel, and last being put aside and finished only rather grudgingly. Mara, the counterpart of Mary Scudder, is the child, and later the woman naturally endowed with grace. The deep currents of Puritanism seem not to affect or disturb Mara. Her religious life is almost wholly a matter of impulse and intuition, not deduction from the Bible. Her fiancé is worldly, but Mara never is in great anxiety about the ultimate state of his soul; she feels sure he will sometime awaken, or be forgiven, or both. Faced with the certainty of an early death from consumption, Mara overcomes fear, despair, resentment, and not too convincingly goes willingly to God. This is not the submission of the Puritan to the will of God so much as it is the impulsively religious person's dying, instead of living, in harmony with the universe, and since the effect does not really come off, the sentimental influence seems strong.

Mrs. Stowe's sense of realism did a few good things here with scenes and characters of the Maine coast, such as Captain Pennel, Miss Ruey, and Miss Roxy. But the story is heavily overlaid with deaths and funerals, so much so that in the early chapters they begin to appear ridiculous.

Maine coastal towns are, and were, old communities as such things go in North America; there is within them a highly delicate balance of friendships and feuds, of irritations and tolerances, and an almost daily, and only partly conscious, casting up of accounts, adjustment, and minute compensation. Such towns are as subtly and finely stratified into social levels as any Yankee city. Probably they were the same in the nineteenth century. Change scarcely touched them until the advent of electricity and the internal combustion engine about the time of World War I, and for twenty years after they showed considerable resistance to innovation. A writer can pick and choose, even in such small places, and find whatever kind of thing he or she wants to look for.

There is much in a place like Orr's Island that Mrs. Stowe's sense of realism never grasped because she was not there long enough, and came, when she did, as a visitor. She was aware of vulgar people there, as elsewhere in the world, but when she used them as a device to threaten young Moses with temptation, she had no real feeling for what she was describing. Less prudish than many of her contemporaries, Mrs. Stowe was still bound to a considerable extent by Victorian gentility, and was insulated emotionally and physically from that amiable, wrily amused, Prince Hal-Falstaff atmosphere that abounds near the wharves and workshops of such coastal towns. When she has Mara crawl through the woods and spy upon the crowd of lower-level near criminals who have enticed Moses out on a drunk, she fails as miserably as any of the lady novelists of her time might. We may value *The Pearl* for some of its sketches, but the strong currents of some of her other books are not in it; it seems to break somewhere in the middle and lose a species of idyllic tone that got underway when the flurry of deaths at the beginning was over. As a novel it falls short of success.

With *Oldtown Folks*, 1869, Mrs. Stowe did some of her best writing about New England, despite certain sentimental overtones already discussed. Thanks probably to her husband's story-telling ability, she seemed to know Oldtown of 1800 (Natick, Massachusetts) much better than she did Orr's Island of 1852. The characters, the descriptions of village life, the humor, are a delight to the reader. Her sense of realism on its own ground and with her own kind of people operates at its best. But the conflict that created the theme of *The Minister's Wooing* is not now centered on any one character. Esther, who is potentially such a character, does not figure so largely in the story as does Tina, a girl who can easily dismiss from her mind such things as she does not wish to see or hear. Without the focus on a sharp, central problem, with at best a rambling form, Mrs. Stowe writes in *Oldtown Folks* a novel that is less excellent than *The Minister's Wooing*, a circumstance which is regrettable, for this fascinating sociological warehouse might have been the better of the two.

She returns in it to the struggle of Puritan theology with certain tenets of the romantic movement. The conflict continues not only within, but also between characters. Grandmother Badger, we are told, holds forth on good Calvinist theology, the while she practices forgiveness, tolerance, mercy, and love; and Grandfather Badger sits in the kitchen poking holes in her logic. Esther is so strained by the strength of her impulses and the rigidity of her sharp, logical thought that she lives as if she were a taut, quivering wife. She is "one of those intense, silent, repressed women that have been a frequent outgrowth of New England society."[22] Mr. Avery, the minister in Cloudland, is a Puritan whose preaching is described as "manly."

22. H. B. Stowe, *Oldtown Folks*, p. 436.

Harriet Beecher Stowe:

Mr. Avery not only preached these things in the pulpit, but talked them out in his daily life. His system of theology was to him the vital breath of his being. His mind was always running upon it, and to it. In his farming, gardening, hunting, or fishing, he was constantly finding new and graphic forms of presenting his favorite truths. The most abstract subject ceased to be abstract in his treatment of it, but became clothed upon with the homely, every-day similes of common life.

I have the image of the dear good man now, as I have seen him, seated on a hay-cart, mending a hoe-handle, and at the same moment vehemently explaining to an inquiring brother minister the exact way that Satan first came to fall, as illustrating how a perfectly holy mind can be tempted to sin.[23]

The Calvinist spokesman is not unattractively presented. He gains an affectionate respect, despite the author's amusement at his innocent reliance on logic to move souls.

My friend's forte is logic. Between you and me, if there is a golden calf worshipped in our sanctified New England, its name is Logic; and my good friend the parson burns incense before it with a most sacred innocence of intention. He believes that sinners can be converted by logic, and that, if he could once get me into one of these neat little traps aforesaid, the salvation of my soul would be assured.[24]

While there is a little gentle spoofing of Calvinist hair-splitting, even the town humorist, Sam Lawson, being given his turn at describing the impossible predicament of the Puritan soul, Calvinism is granted frequent passages of praise and credit:

---

23. *Ibid.*, p. 442.
24. *Ibid.*, p. 224.

For this set of shrewd, toil-hardened, vigorous, full-blooded republicans I can think of no preaching more admirably adapted than Mr. Avery's. It was preaching that was on the move, as their minds were, and which was slowly shaping out and elaborating those new forms of society. Living, as these men did, a lonely, thoughtful, secluded life ... their two Sunday sermons were the great intellectual stimulus which kept their minds bright, and they were listened to with an intense interest of which the scattered and diversified stage of modern society gives few examples. They felt the compliment of being talked to as if they were capable of understanding the very highest of subjects, and they liked it. Each hard, heroic nature flashed like a flint at the thought of free agency with which not even their Maker would interfere. Their God himself asked to reign over them not by force, but by the free, voluntary choice of their own hearts. . . .[25]

Grandmother Badger, speaking of the clear, luke-warm, and sensible sermons of her minister in Oldtown, says:

"They are good as far as they go . . . but I like good, strong, old-fashioned doctrine. I like such writers as Mr. Edwards and Dr. Bellamy and Dr. Hopkins. It's all very well, your essays on cheerfulness and resignation and all that; but I want something that takes strong hold of you, so that you feel something has got you that *can* hold."[26]

And Jonathan Rossiter writes to his sister, "I am not one of the shallow sort, who think that everything for everybody must or ought to end with perfect bliss at death." But the wedge has been driven just the same. Of Mr. Avery, a character modelled on Lyman

25. *Ibid.*, p. 447.
26. *Ibid.*, pp. 74-75.

Beecher, Jonathan Rossiter writes his sister:

> My good friend preaches what they call New
> Divinity, by which I understand the Calvinism which
> our fathers left us, in the commencing process of
> disintegration. He is thoroughly and enthusiastically
> in earnest about it, and believes that the system, as
> far as Edwards and Hopkins have got it, is almost
> absolute truth; but, for all that, is cheerfully busy in
> making some little emendations and corrections, upon
> which he values himself, and which he thinks of the
> greatest consequence. What is to the credit of his
> heart is that these emendations are generally in favor
> of some original-minded sheep who can't be got into
> the sheep-fold without some alteration in the paling.
> In these cases I have generally noticed that he will
> loosen a rail or tear off a picket, and let the sheep in, it
> being his impression, after all, that the sheep are
> worth more than the sheep-fold.[27]

And Mehitable Rossiter, discussing a very
different and obviously much sterner Calvinist
preacher of some years back in Oldtown reports:

> His theory was that a secret enemy to God was
> lying latent in every soul, which, like some virulent
> poisons in the body, could only be expelled by being
> brought to the surface; and he had sermon after
> sermon, whose only object appeared to be to bring into
> vivid consciousness what he calls the natural
> opposition of the human heart.[28]

Both Emily Rossiter and Ellery Davenport are so
alienated by Calvinist doctrine that they have bolted
down a path lined with Rousseau-esque primroses.
Esther's emotions are unhealthily contained by her
intense intellectuality, and her salvation comes only

---

27. *Ibid.*, p. 223.
28. *Ibid.*, p. 215.

---

through the love of Harry, a lad whose intuitive
doctrine, like Mary Scudder's, takes its cue from the
heart and establishes a loving and forgiving God:

> "the difference between Esther and myself is just the
> reverse kind of that which generally subsists between
> man and woman. She has been all her life so drilled in
> what logicians call reasoning, that although she has a
> glorious semi-spiritual nature, and splendid moral
> instincts, she never trusts them. She is like an eagle
> that should insist upon climbing a mountain by beak
> and claw instead of using wings. She must always see
> the syllogism before she will believe."
>   "You always speak of Christ as God."
>   "I have never thought of God in any other way," he
> answered. ". . . those who learn religion by sorrow
> always turn to him. . . ."[29]

Talk like this is a long step from the old
Puritanism. By the time Mrs. Stowe wrote *Oldtown
Folks*, she had joined the Episcopal Church. Harry, at
the close of the novel, has gone to England and
become an Episcopal rector. Throughout the book, the
heart's reasons that the head knows nothing of
become ascendant. Goody Smith, the Badgers, Miss
Mehitable, Tina, Mr. Avery—all are swinging away from
deduction from premises as a guide to human action,
and respond to deep-rooted emotion. The world,
including Mrs. Stowe, *has* deserted Calvinism, but this
is a painful thing for her to admit even ten years after
The Minister's Wooing, and besides she does not wish
to be misunderstood: so many people have slid away
from the old faith casually and lightly into nothing that
she feels a necessity to explain the serious spirit of her
move. Her position is like that of the person who is too

---

29. *Ibid.*, pp. 520-521.

---

religious to attend church and dislikes to be confused with those who abstain merely from laziness.

The casual drift into an earnest materialism under a cake-icing of respectable piety, which Mrs. Stowe saw in the seventies, may have induced her to turn her attention to the surface abuses of wealth.

Although repeatedly she had subscribed in other novels to the wisdom, nay even the duty, of following one's deep-rooted instincts and intuitions, she was revolted, as many an artist and philosopher has been, by the shallow exploitation of these truths for self-indulgence and irresponsibility. Her impulses, as well as her training, told her such self-indulgence was immoral, and her sense of gentility told her in no uncertain terms it was disreputable. The path between license and psychic harmony was, after all, narrow, and Mrs. Stowe hastened to cry in *Pink and White Tyranny*: "That was not what I meant. That was not what I meant at all!"

The book, her attempt at an American *Vanity Fair*, attacks a frivolous and silly social life for the damage it does to human character. Lillie Ellis, self-centered and calculating, quite simply marries for money and makes a poor bargain for a decent but ingenuous New Englander. She goes quite a way toward spoiling his life, flirts with adultery, and rather regretfully bears some children. The surgery of divorce, even for extreme cases of maladjustment, is beyond the pale in Mrs. Stowe's mind, and she has John Seymour learn gradually what his wife is like and then make the best of it. But Seymour is too simple and in a way too shallow a character to lend much significance or depth to the book. Besides, the daily habits of both the virtuous, Connecticut mill-owning family and of the silly socialites fall considerably short of the good life. Lillie Ellis and friends act on the tedious "have-fun" fallacy, while the Sunday-school teaching, priggish New Englanders go for bird walks, "Oh-ing" and "Ah-ing" over Nature and smugly expounding against French art, the while they indulge in charity and abstain from basic economic reforms.

One should give credit to Mrs. Stowe, however, for being willing to write about a romance that turns sour. The discouraging fact is that in this novel, as well as in *My Wife and I* and *We and Our Neighbors*, the reader feels that earnest attention is expended on elements in life not worth the effort. The three books lack the strength to be found in her others; their issues seem somehow trivial contrasted to the serious probing of *The Minister's Wooing*. New England gets into *My Wife and I* and *Pink and White Tyranny*, but not much of it, and although Mrs. Stowe obviously knows something about the various sections of New York and the editorial offices there, she does not know them with bone and sinew as she does Oldtown.

My Wife and I and *We and Our Neighbors* are accounts of the happy courtships and early married life of decorous and not extraordinary New Englanders in New York City. The Van Arsdels, Harry Henderson, and their friends, in their customary lives, financial gains and losses, troubles with relatives, and so on, indicate a series of minor morals, all well enough, but not in such a manner as to convince one of significant writing or of reality either. The reader comes from these books aware he has been told, but perhaps not shown, that selfish, unloving women are created by a shallow society and make poor wives, that some rich people lead silly lives, that high church Episcopalians and Roman Catholics are, after all, religious and one should be glad of it, that society in its bigoted moods drives erring girls to prostitution instead of giving them merciful help, that alcoholism is a horrifying failing, that one should be kind to dogs, tolerant of bothersome relatives, content with moderate income, and thoroughly interested in some useful thinking outside oneself. Certain of these subjects have provided serviceable themes for literary works, and there is not necessarily anything wrong with many of them. A few might be used as starting points for good fiction, but Mrs. Stowe sprinkled them throughout a relatively light treatment. Here and there a remaining wisp of Puritanism turns up in Ida or Caroline of *My Wife and I*, but the great issue seems dead and so do the characters and themes. Any stray currents from the romantic movement produce little force in these books, although original goodness is in every character, particularly in the misled. The sense of realism to be found in some of Mrs. Stowe's other works is only occasionally uppermost, and although the plot of *Pink and White Tyranny* is far from the old sentimental pattern, the sentimental clichés of the threatened adultery, the extended epistolary form, and overdone phraseology in underdone situations are present in all three novels. The most one can say is that Mrs. Stowe attacked some elements of 1870 life that warranted the attack. She did not, however, plunge deep; neither did she create much convincing fiction.

Reminiscent is the word for Mrs. Stowe's swan

song as a novelist, *Poganuc People*, 1878, a nostalgic and charming return to the New England country village of the early nineteenth century. With a sure hand she depicts the childhood and growth of Dolly Cushing, a more or less autobiographical little girl, in a thinly disguised Litchfield, Connecticut. Until the appearance of a few clichés in the final chapters, which Mrs. Stowe hastens through as she ever tends to do with her closing pages, the book is relatively free of the curse of the sentimental. Nabbie and Seth Higgins are successfully convincing and memorable characters. Especially so is the picture of Zeph on election day, so careful of his independent vote that he can be handled almost too easily. He was, the author says:

> born to oppose, as much as white bears are made to walk on ice. And how, we ask, would New England's rocky soil and icy hills have been made mines of wealth unless there had been human beings born to oppose, delighting to combat and wrestle, and with an unconquerable power of will?[30]

Parson Cushing, like Mr. Avery of *Oldtown Folks*, is modelled on Lyman Beecher and his dismay over the election of 1818 that turned to toleration, separating church and state in Connecticut, transmits itself to the child, Dolly:

> It was with a voice tremulous and choking with emotion that Dr. Cushing thus poured forth the fears and sorrows of his heart for the New England of the Puritans: the ideal church and state which they came hither to found.
> Little Dolly cried from a strange childish fear because of the trouble in her father's voice. The

---

30. H. B. Stowe, *Poganuc People*, p. 65.

---

pleading tones affected her, she knew not why . . .
after prayers Dolly climbed into her father's lap, and
put both arms around his neck, and said, "Papa, there
sha'nt anything hurt you. I'll defend you." She was
somewhat abashed by the cheerful laugh which
followed. . . .[31]

Much of the charm, joy, and sorrow of Beecher
biography gets into this novel: the nutting expeditions,
the vigorous and almost holy Fourth of July
celebrations, the rambling Beecher house with its rats
and cats who live in a state of mutual security, the
beauty and excitement of changing seasons, and the
grim tolling of the New England church bell, one
stroke for each year of the deceased's life. Nor is the
familiar struggle over Puritanism absent. Out of life-
long respect, out of attachment to the God of her
father, and out of a suspicion that something, on the
whole, admirable has passed out of the world in her
time, Mrs. Stowe salutes it yet again:

Never was there a freer rationalism than in the
inquiries which the New England theology tolerated
and encouraged at every fireside.[32]

If Mrs. Stowe was growing tired and ready for a
nostalgic mood, she had a right to be by 1877, not
only because of her age, but also because of her
literary output, the storms raised over *Uncle Tom's
Cabin* and *Lady Byron Vindicated*, the violent deaths of
her brother George, her son Henry, and the alcoholism
and disappearance of her wounded son, Frederick.
Wordsworth, after all, in his day had ceased
struggling, decided not to be a pagan suckled in a

31. *Ibid.*, pp. 72-73.
32. *Ibid.*, p. 173.

creed outworn, and rested in the fold of the Anglican Church.

Dolly Cushing in *Poganuc People* makes a quiet, gentle, and painless shift from her father's Calvinism toward the Episcopal Church. Even as a little girl she runs off at night to attend a Christmas illumination in the new Episcopal chapel because the decorations are so pretty, and her father, discovering this misbehavior, promptly forgives her.

Biographers have interpreted this quite credibly as Mrs. Stowe's guaranteeing herself the forgiveness she feels the need of from a father figure. C.H. Foster points out that in return, little Dolly brings the recalcitrant Zeph Higgins back into the fold of the Calvinist faith, so that something, in a symbolic sense, has been done to repay Lyman Beecher.[33]

To conclude from these books that the romantic movement downed Calvinism and drove people to the Episcopal Church would be extreme and ridiculous. The latter it simply did not do, of course. But it is not going too far to say that two powerful world-views, Calvinism and romanticism, which penetrated to every part of life, personal, social, political, religious, and economic could not equally hold sway in American society. The seeds of the romantic movement had been long deep and dormant. Even Jonathan Edwards' writings of mystical experience in the presence of flowers and trees on a New England hillside have about them a touch of what was to become a romantic viewpoint. E. D. Branch goes so far as to suggest a

---

33. C. H. Foster, p. 240.

---

biochemical cause for the violent shift of outlook:

> Romantic thought entered the United States in three
> ways, and possibly by a fourth; for it may be that
> general endoglandular changes are effected (as great
> climatic changes occur) by forces which biochemists
> have not yet charted.[34]

Whatever the cause, Mrs. Stowe lived, grew, and wrote during some crucial years of struggle; the drama of the change, and results of the change are integral parts of her novels. It was even her destiny to help force the decline of the old religion (just as it had been Lyman Beecher's too, and was Henry Ward's, and Catherine's) and Mrs. Stowe did not relish thinking of it; but given her deep psychic response to impulse, to intuition, given the society in which she lived, one is inclined to think that in this respect she had little free agency. The Episcopal Church was for her an acceptable haven from the torments of the storm. Not only could she accept it but she could take it earnestly and seriously, more earnestly and seriously, she felt, than some who had had it all along and were only respectably pious.

> When I said, "I should think those who hear and say
> such glorious things at church ought to live the very
> noblest lives, . . ." he said, "Cousin, I am sorry to say it
> is not so with me. We hear these things from
> childhood; we hear them Sunday after Sunday, in all
> sorts of moods, and I'm afraid many of us form a habit
> of not really thinking how much they mean. I wish I
> could hear our service as you have done, for the first
> time, and that it would seem as real and earnest to me
> as it does to you."[35]

---

34. E. D. Branch, p. 325.
35. H. B. Stowe, *Poganuc People*, p. 257.

Woman and Artist

Poganuc People is a novel of which Mrs. Stowe had no need to be ashamed, and it is thoroughly fitting as her last. Today the crudity and carelessness of much of her craftsmanship harshly scores our reader's sense, while we calmly forget or push aside a mass of poor writing in our own time. Our literary history is the richer for having had one more writer who was able to rise as much as she did above the contemporary cloud of shallow sentiment; whose sense of realism could clash with the ideal and precipitate humor; who could write two novels of social protest, one of them influential enough to turn the head of any writer, and still go on to novels that probed the nature of Nature (the role of all significant art), that recorded the tensions and conflicts of a soul caught between opposing views of the universe. Whether one can accept her beliefs is beside the point. She was acutely conscious, at least, that there were more topics worthy of discussion than sports, courtship, and subsistence. In an ironical mood she once wrote:

> "This is the victory that overcometh the world"—to learn to be fat and tranquil, to have warm fires and good dinners, to hang your hat on the same peg at the same hour every day, to sleep soundly all night, and never to trouble your head with a thought or imagining beyond.[36]

There was a victory to which Harriet Beecher Stowe never remotely stooped. She was profoundly, and just as profoundly when she was humorously, *serieuse.*

It is time the world stopped thinking "blood-

---

36. H. B. Stowe, *The Minister's Wooing*, p. 118.

hounds" or "Eliza" in conditioned response to her name, and turned to her books to experience the depths, summits, hurdles, and hazards of her fragment of the eternal search.

GALLERY

1. HARRIET BEECHER STOWE
(Hall of Fame bust by Brenda Putnam)

2. AN IMAGINATIVE LIKENESS OF MRS. STOWE.
Note the odd placement of the book's title

Richmond, Del.   J.A.J.Wilcox Sc.

3. MRS. STOWE IN HER THIRTIES

4. THE HAWES DAGUERROTYPE

Eng^d by A. H. Ritchie.

Harriet Beecher Stowe

5. IN MIDDLE AGE

6. IN LATER YEARS

7. THE BEECHER FAMILY—1855
Standing (l to r): Thomas, William, Edward, Charles, Henry Ward.
Seated: Isabella, Catherine, Lyman Beecher, Mary, Harriet. Inset:
James. (portrait by Matthew Brady.)

8. CALVIN ELLIS STOWE
Harriet's husband

9. THE LANE FACULTY IN THE 1840S
Calvin Ellis Stowe   Lyman Beecher   D.H. Allen

10. THE STOWE HOUSE IN BRUNSWICK, MAINE
where *Uncle Tom's Cabin* was written

Uncle Tom

The cabin of Uncle Tom was a small log building close adjoining to "the house" — as the negro always par excellence designates the masters dwelling — In front it had a neat garden patch where strawberries raspberries & a variety of fruits [& vegetables] flourished under careful tending — down The whole front of the dwelling was covered with a large[r] big[scarlet] nonia & a native multiflora rose which entwisting & interlacing left scarce a vestage of the building to be seen & in the spring was redundant with its clusters of roses & in summer no less brilliant with the scarlet tubes of the bignonia Various gay brilliant annuals such as marigolds four o'clocks & petunias found here and there a thrifty corner to vegetate unfold their glories & were the delight & pride of aunt Chloe's heart

Let us enter the dwelling — The evening meal at "the house" is over & Aunt Chloe who presides over its preparation as head cook has left to inferior officers in the kitchen the business of clearing away & washing dishes & come out into her own snug territory to "get her old man's supper" & therefore doubt not that it is her you see by the fire place presiding with anxious interest

11. A MANUSCRIPT PAGE FROM *UNCLE TOM'S CABIN*

BIBLIOGRAPHY

Bradford, Gameliel, *Portraits of American Women*, Boston, Houghton Mifflin Co., 1919.

Branch, Douglas E., *The Sentimental Years*, New York, D. Appleton-Century Co., Inc., 1934.

Brown, Herbert Ross, *The Sentimental Novel in America, 1789-1860*, Durham, N.C., Duke University Press, 1940.

Cooper, James Fenimore, *The Wing-and-Wing*, New York, Belford Clarke & Company, 1887.

Donovan, Josephine, *New England Local Color Literature*, Ungar Publishing Co., New York, 1983.

Fiedler, Leslie, *An End to Innocence*, Boston, The Beacon Press, 1955.

Fields, Annie, editor, *The Life and Letters of Harriet Beecher Stowe*, Boston, Houghton Mifflin and Co., 1898.

Foster, Charles H., *The Rungless Ladder*, Durham, N.C. Duke University Press, 1954.

Foster, Hannah Webster, *The Coquette*, Boston, William Fetridge and Co., 1855.

Fullerton, B.M., *Selective Bibliography of American Literature, 1775-1900*, New York, William Farquhar Payson, 1932.

Gilbertson, Catherine, *Harriet Beecher Stowe*, D. Appleton-Century Co., Inc., 1937.

Howard, John Tucker, *Our American Music*, New York, Thomas Y. Crowell, 1931.

Kelley, Mary, *Private Women, Public Stage: Literary Domesticity in Nineteenth Century America*, New York, Oxford University Press, 1984.

LaFever, Minard, *The Modern Builder's Guide*, New York, Paine & Burgess, 1846.

Mattfield, Julius, *Variety Music Cavalcade*, New York, Prentice-Hall, 1952.

Miller, Perry, *Jonathan Edwards*, New York, William Sloane Associates, Inc., 1949.

Minnegerode, Meade, *The Fabulous Forties*, New York, G.P. Putnam's Sons, 1924.

Neuhaus, Eugen, *The History and Ideals of American Art*, Stanford University, California, Stanford University Press, 1931.

Pattee, Fred Lewis, *The Feminine Fifties*, New York, Funk and Wagnalls, Co., 1905.

Saint Gaudens, Homer, *The American Artist and His Time*, New York, Dodd Mead and Co., 1941.

Starkey, Marion L., *The Devil in Massachusetts*, New York, Alfred A. Knopf, 1950.

Stowe, Charles Edward and Lyman Beecher, *Harriet Beecher Stowe*, Boston, Hougton Mifflin Co., 1911.

Stowe, Harriet Beecher, *Agnes of Sorrento*, Boston, Ticknor and Fields, 1862.

——————————————, *Dred, A Tale of the Great Dismal Swamp*, two volumes, Boston, Phillips Sampson & Co., 1856.

——————————————, *The Minister's Wooing*, New York, Derby and Jackson, 1859.

——————————————, *My Wife and I*, Boston, D. Lothrop & Co., 1871.

——————————————, *Oldtown Folks*, Boston, Houghton Mifflin and Co., 1986. *1896?*

——————————————, —*The Pearl of Orr's Island*, Boston, Houghton Mifflin and Co., 1986. *1896?* *original dates of publication would be useful*

——————————————, *Pink and White Tyranny*, Boston, Houghton Mifflin Co., 1918.

——————————————, *Poganuc People*, Boston, Houghton Mifflin Co., 1913.

————————————, *Uncle Tom's Cabin*, Boston, Houghton Mifflin Co., two volumes, 1892.

————————————, *We and Our Neighbors*, Boston, D. Lothrop & Co. 1875.

Ticknor, Caroline, *Hawthorne and his Publisher*, Boston, Houghton Mifflin and Co., 1913.

Tompkins, Jane, *Sensational Designs: The Cultural Work of American Fiction 1790-1860*, New York, Oxford University Press, 1985.

Wector, Dixon, *The Saga of American Society*, New York, Charles Scribner's Sons, 1957.

Whitman, Walter, *Franklin Evans, or The Inebriate*, New York, Random House (Merrymount Press edition, Boston), 1929.

Wilson, Forrest, *Crusader in Crinoline*, New York, J.P. Lippincott, Co., 1941.

INDEX

Publisher's Note

Harriet Beecher Stowe: Woman and Artist is the first book in a new series concerned to bring belated reassessment to a number of great women writers who, in a male dominated society, have not been given the kind of recognition they so richly deserve. This neglect may have been unintentional, but it has created critical lacunae which should be corrected.

We believe that we are entering a new era almost as significant as that which finally brought women's suffrage into being with the 19th amendment. How many people know that the movement for women's rights in Europe was started in Norway during the 1880s with the help of Sigrid Undset, author of *Kristin Lavrensdatter?* If it had not been for her work, Ibsen would not have raised the questions he raised in *A Doll's House* and other plays. It used to be said that the sound of the door Nora slammed at the end of that play echoed all over Europe. We can say now it also echoed around the world. Certainly, if it were not for Ibsen's concerns with the "battle of the sexes", Strindberg would not have taken up the challenge in *The Father* and other plays inspired by a virulent anti-female bias. But that bias was so outrageous and he so clearly psychotic that the work back-fired and he in effect advanced the cause. Then Shaw, whose introduced Ibsen and Strindberg to the west and became invaluable grist for the mills of Susan B. Anthony and Elizabeth Cady Stanton. These pioneers had been working for more than forty years for such basic women's causes as the legal right to own property, to have something to say about their own children, and finally the right to vote. Although the mills of justice grind slowly, the time has now come for renewed dedication. *and better proofreading*

Hannah Arendt once said that it takes three generations to change ingrained social attitudes. Lincoln's Emancipation Proclamation was only a first step in a process by no means complete. Laws may be passed, but the real revolution must take place by raising the consciousness of the public. Or, as John Adams said about America's fight for freedom, "the revolution took place in the minds of the people."

In thinking about these things some 30 years ago, I used the phrase "*mortmain* [the dead, hence heavy, hand] of the past." In any cultural ethos, the attitudes of the past weigh heavily. The hard-won fight for a Civil Rights Bill in the 1960s was a great step forward, but still the movement toward equal rights for blacks and all ethnic groups has a long way to go. Still, progress is being made, and the time will come when all the children of whatever gods there be will be free.

Surely, Harriet Beecher Stowe is an prime victim of the mid-nineteenth century bias that still prevails. She was the greatest and most significant American novelist of her time, greater than any of those who preceded her, such as Charles Brockden Brown, Hawthorne, Irving, etc. And as Holmes demonstrates, her whole life's work has been overshadowed by *Uncle Tom's Cabin.* And in our time, even that book has been neglected in favor of Melville. But the tide will turn yet.

The idea that Melville was a great novelist occurred almost by accident quite recently. Before WWI, universities offered courses in English Literature, but none about the books written by Americans. Since during WWI we had gone all out to "make the world safe for democracy," why not make the world aware of American writers? To do so, they imported not only ideas for works to study, but also the European anti-woman biases that dictated critical judgements at the time: biases that led Mary Ann Evans to call herself George Eliot and Armadine Dupin to call herself George Sand. In that spirit, all hands concerned went looking for a man. In the hunt, comeone discovered that Melville had been born in 1819. So to celebrate his centennial, they dug up *Moby Dick*, a book that had not been mentioned by anybody for fifty years. Melville was declared to be the greatest American novelist of his time. *De gustibus non disputandum est.*

Harriet Beecher Stowe: Woman and Artist will clearly show that Melville was not alone in the running. She had a mind that grasped significance, eyes that could see, and ears that could hear. Someone has said if a person would like to know about the culture and social mores of French society during the first half of the nineteenth century, he should go first to the work of Balzac. Balzac knew well what he was doing and called his dozens of novels chapters in a big design he called "The Human Comedy." He was using the word in the Dantescan sense of drama, and not as something funny. The same can be said of the human condition in Russia at the same time. Books about Czars and Czarinas tell little, while the works of Dostoevsky and Tolstoy tell all.

So with Harriet Beecher Stowe. With the nicest of art she gives us insights into the human condition of her time. And in so doing, she gives us all a challenge. We must face the fact that our media masters are mental, spiritual and moral idiots. We must seek out the great neglected women writers of the past and see to it that they get their due. We must rise to the occasion and use the media to make progress toward the final goal of liberation and equal treatment for all.

—Carroll F. Terrell